Mayor
Crump
Don't Like It

Contents

Mayor
Crump
Don't Like It

Machine Politics in Memphis

G. Wayne Dowdy

University Press of Mississippi / *Jackson*

www.upress.state.ms.us

The University Press of Mississippi is a member of the
Association of American University Presses.

First edition 2006
∞
Library of Congress Cataloging-in-Publication Data

Dowdy, G. Wayne.
    Mayor Crump don't like it : machine politics in Memphis / G. Wayne Dowdy.— 1st ed.
      p. cm.
    Includes bibliographical references and index.
    ISBN 1-57806-859-2 (cloth : alk. paper) 1. Crump, Edward Hull, 1874–1954.
2. Mayors—Tennessee—Memphis—Biography. 3. Politics, Practical—Tennessee—
Memphis—History—20th century. 4. Memphis (Tenn.)—Politics and government—20th century. 5. African Americans—Tennessee—Memphis—Politics and
government—20th century. 6. Memphis (Tenn.)—Race relations—History—20th
century. 7. Memphis (Tenn.)—Biography. 8. Legislators—United States—Biography.
9. United States Congress. House—Biography. I. Title.
    F444.M553C783 2006
    976.8'19053092—dc22   2005026409

British Library Cataloging-in-Publication Data available

Foreword

"Plan Your Work and Work Your Plan"

On a cold winter's day in 1894, nineteen-year-old Edward Hull Crump of Holly Springs, Mississippi, boarded a train for Memphis, the unofficial capital of the Mid-South and the logical destination for country people seeking a better life. Taking his seat, the young man perhaps reflected on his past as the locomotive pulled out of the station and headed toward the big city. Born near Holly Springs on October 2, 1874, Crump grew to adulthood within the remnants of the planter class that had led the South for generations. His father, also named Edward Hull Crump, was a cotton planter and Confederate army officer who died during the yellow fever epidemic of 1878.[1]

The elder Crump left behind his wife, Mollie Nelms, three children, of which Edward was the youngest, and land that needed to be worked. Mollie Nelms Crump was a stubborn, sometimes inflexible woman, tempered with a sense of humor. When Crump was mayor, his mother rebuked him for his attack on a political rival: "I must tell you how mortified I was when I read that article in the evening paper. I could not sleep to think my son would use such language. Where did you learn it? . . . No one else writes as you do and I am ashamed of you. . . ."[2] Upon her husband's death she did her best to take care of the family farm and her children, but poverty dogged them at every

ix

turn. The example of a headstrong mother struggling to keep her family out of the poorhouse had a profound effect on young Edward. These childhood experiences created within him an abiding faith in organization and a fiery determination to succeed in life. "Plan your work and work your plan," was his favorite platitude. When the train pulled into the Illinois Central station at Memphis, Crump walked through the downtown district, determined to be a success.[3]

Positioned atop the fourth Chickasaw bluff overlooking the Mississippi River, Memphis was the largest city in the Mid-South and that region's distribution center. The city was founded by land speculators Andrew Jackson, John Overton, and James Winchester in 1819. Because of its position on the river, the town became a market for agricultural goods, especially cotton, grown in the rural communities of north Mississippi, eastern Arkansas, and western Tennessee. An increase in agricultural production and the construction of the Memphis/Charleston Railroad made Memphis the fastest-growing city in the United States during the 1850s. During the Civil War the Bluff City escaped the destruction visited upon other southern commercial centers owing to its quick surrender to Union forces in June 1862.[4]

Its position as a distribution center was exploited by northern merchants whose goods (both legal and illegal) flowed through the city and strengthened the local economy.[5] When the war ended, thousands of newly freed slaves moved into the Irish-dominated southern sections of the city, which exacerbated the crime, overcrowding, and unemployment indicative of the poorer sections of Memphis. Hostility between the Irish, African Americans, and former Confederate soldiers erupted into violence in May 1866 when Irish police officers and black Union troops fought a pitched battle over several days. Forty-four African Americans and two white rioters died in the melee.[6] The 1866 race riot solidified for many the image of Memphis as a raucous, violence-prone city. An editorial writer for the *New York Mercury*

Acknowledgments

In writing this book I received from colleagues, family, and friends a great deal of encouragement and support which can never be adequately repaid. History department senior manager Dr. James R. Johnson and former archivist Dr. Barbara D. Flanary unfailingly encouraged me to pursue the study of Memphis history, while the administration of the Memphis Public Library and Information Center, director Judith A. Drescher, deputy director Sallie Johnson, and central public services manager Kay Mills Due, supported that encouragement.

Gina Cordell, Gregg L. Newby, and Patrick W. O'Daniel of the Memphis Public Library's history department greatly assisted me in preparing the manuscript for publication. In addition, the rest of the history department staff—Betty Blaylock, Joan Cannon, Robert C. Cruthirds, Stephanie DeClue, Doris G. Dixon, Leslie W. Hirsch, Thomas W. Jones, Patricia M. LaPointe, Donald B. Strickland, Belmar Toney, and Marilyn Umfrees—supported my research and endured endless conversations about Mr. Crump. Other library staff members who deserve mention are Christina Barnes, Susan Berry, Freda Hopkins, Stephanie Masin, Gina Milburn, Ruth Morrison, Melissa Skipper, Nathan Tipton, and Philip Williams.

Noted scholars Charles W. Crawford, Timothy S. Huebner, Bobby L. Lovett, and Robert A. Sigafoos each in his own way encouraged me to write this monograph. I also wish to thank Craig W. Gill, editor-in-chief of the University Press of Mississippi, who nurtured this project from its inception, and Melvin G. Holli, who read the entire manuscript and offered insightful comments which improved the final outcome. Portions of this book appeared in *Arkansas Review: A Journal of Delta Studies*, *CrossRoads: A Southern Culture Annual*, *Tennessee Historical Quarterly*, and *West Tennessee Historical Society Papers*. I thank John E. Harkins, Marc A. Jolley, Ann Toplovich, and Thomas S. Williams for their generous permission to use the previously published material.

More importantly, I could not have completed this task without the love and generosity of my family. I dedicate this book to my parents, Gerald McLain and Barbara Ann Nance Dowdy, my grandparents, John McLain and Ivy Lucile Heckle Dowdy and William Herbert and Lurline Belle Griffin Nance, my brother and sister-in-law, William Johnathan "Bud" and Robin Paige Clement Dowdy, my niece, Britney Amber Dowdy, and my nephews, Cody Austin Dowdy and Brandon Ryan Dowdy.

newspaper summed up this attitude in 1870: "[T]o those weary of life, but who have not the courage to shoot or hang themselves, we recommend a trip to Memphis. . . . All one need do is say 'you lie, you villain' to the first person one meets, and shortly the coroner will announce that your body is doing duty as a corpse."[7]

Wartime prosperity did not last much beyond 1865, as property values declined and the city's bonded indebtedness expanded beyond its ability to pay. Memphis's precarious situation was made worse in 1878 when over five thousand citizens died during an outbreak of yellow fever. These catastrophes forced Memphis into bankruptcy and led to the loss of its municipal charter in 1879. By the time young E. H. Crump arrived in Memphis, the city had for the most part recovered from the devastation of the 1870s. In 1892 the first Mississippi River bridge below St. Louis was built at Memphis, and that same year 770,000 bales of cotton were shipped from the city. Regaining its charter in 1893, Memphis emerged as a leading city of the New South.[8]

Upon his arrival Crump struggled to find a job. He landed temporary positions with a cotton trader and a real estate firm, but it was not until 1896 that he found permanent employment. Crump was hired as a bookkeeper for the Woods Carriage Company, and he quickly climbed the nineteenth-century version of the corporate ladder. Two years later the company merged with a saddle-making concern, forming the Woods-Chickasaw Manufacturing Company, and in 1900 Crump was named secretary/treasurer of the new corporation. In 1902 he married Bessie Byrd McLean, the daughter of one of Memphis's leading businessmen. The year after their marriage, Crump purchased the Woods-Chickasaw company.[9]

His skills as a businessman, which were considerable, were subsumed, however, by his passion for politics. Exactly when he first developed a taste for public affairs is not known, but it initially manifested itself when Crump was elected director of the Memphis

Business Men's Club in 1904. The most important decision Crump made in his debut electoral effort was in appointing insurance agent and Spanish-American War veteran Frank Rice campaign manager. A brilliant political operator, Rice emerged as Crump's most trusted advisor.[10] Becoming director of the Business Men's Club was significant for Crump in another way. There he came into contact with many of Memphis's leading progressives, including attorney Kenneth D. McKellar. Association with these reformers sparked Crump's interest and broadened his understanding of local politics. In 1905 McKellar and other progressives agitated successfully to amend the city charter to make it more accountable to the people. The amended document weakened the power of the mayor and expanded the size of the city council.[11]

Crump was not involved in the charter fight, but his belief in municipal reform led him to run for a seat on the board of public works supervisors, the lower body of the bicameral legislative council. Rice managed the campaign while Crump introduced himself to voters by embarking on a door-to-door tour of Memphis neighborhoods. Responding to this personal touch, voters elected Crump by an overwhelming majority.[12] Election to the legislative council set the young Mississippian on a path that led him to great power and influence.

Over the next fifty-four years Crump built one of the greatest, and most diverse, political organizations in American history. In amassing political dominion over the Mississippi Delta's largest city, Crump employed tactics almost unheard of in the American South. He created a biracial, multiethnic coalition which brought special-interest politics to the Jim Crow South. In so doing he not only acquired great power, but also helped change the course of the national Democratic Party. How Crump did this uncovers the hitherto unknown diversity of southern politics and its influence on the American political landscape.

Mayor
Crump
Don't Like It

"A Business Government
by a Business Man"

On January 4, 1906, Crump began his long political career when he was sworn in as a member of the board of public works supervisors. Wasting little time, the new supervisor challenged the status quo operation of city government by demanding the elimination of waste and the adoption of several reform measures. These included increasing the amount of license fees paid by saloons, the strict adherence to a competitive bidding process, and a speed limit for the city's growing number of automobile drivers.[1] Old-line Memphis politicians were not interested in Crump's reforms and blocked him at every turn. They did, however, assign him to chair a committee that oversaw the placement of light poles, which gave him insight into the operation of a private utility.[2] Troubled by his lack of progress on the lower board, Crump abruptly resigned his seat in September 1907 to devote more time to his business interests.[3]

Or so he claimed. The real reason became apparent in October when he announced he was a candidate for a seat on the board of fire and police commissioners. The centerpiece of his campaign was the promise of support for the construction of a city-owned electric light plant, which brought him the endorsement of local progressives. Crump's election to the fire and police commission made him one of the most recognizable reformers in Memphis and he was

3

determined to stay in the public eye. The new fire and police commissioner called for a special meeting immediately after his swearing in on January 2, 1908, where he denounced local law enforcement and ordered police chief George O'Haver to close all saloons by midnight. Later that month Crump personally led raids on gambling dens, which delighted progressives and embarrassed city officials who claimed there was no gambling in Memphis.[4]

The public ownership of utilities and strict law enforcement were matters of great concern to local progressives, but in 1908 the primary issue was the blocking of their reform program by the status quo legislative council. It became clear that the 1905 charter amendments did not go far enough in addressing the inefficient nature of local politics. Crump shared their frustration and joined in their campaign to overhaul city affairs through the adoption of the commission form of government. The commission plan was designed to centralize authority in the hands of a small board of elected officials who were chosen by a city-wide vote and acted as both legislators and department heads.[5] By concentrating power in the hands of a few commissioners, it was thought, government would operate efficiently and be more accountable to the people.

When a commission bill for Memphis was introduced in the Tennessee General Assembly, Commissioner Crump traveled to Nashville and aggressively lobbied for its passage. The bill became law in February 1909, and its passage was attributed in large part to the efforts of the progressive fire and police commissioner.[6] As the city bureaucracy began the transition to a new form of government, Crump weighed his options. He had become a recognized leader in both government and progressive circles and it was not hard for him to conclude that his chances for election to the new commission were high. Furthermore, no one understood the inefficiency of the previous government better than he did. Crump obviously concluded he was better suited than anyone else to serve as the head of Memphis's new government and consequently announced his candidacy for mayor in August 1909. Describing himself as "the foremost advocate of the commission form of government,"[7] Crump promised "a business government by a business man."[8]

Crump was opposed by former mayor J. J. Williams, who controlled a formidable political organization made up of the white working class, African Americans, and saloon owners. Criminal leaders such as George Honan, who murdered a sheriff's deputy during Williams's tenure, were enthusiastic supporters.[9] Progressives despised Williams's brand of politics, especially his alliance with the underworld. They took the elitist view that the political involvement of the working class and blacks corrupted the electoral process. Crump initially shared their outlook and this was reflected in his campaign.

Crump's campaign manager, Frank Rice, placed advertisements in local newspapers that emphasized Williams's relationship with gangsters and charged the former mayor with organizing "crap-shooting negroes, who will sell their vote for a few cents or a drink of mean whiskey."[10] Middle-class progressives were solidly behind Crump but that did not necessarily mean there were enough votes to defeat Williams's working class/African American coalition. In order to excite the voters, both campaigns held rallies on the eve of the election. One thousand people gathered in Gaston Park to hear several speakers promote the Crump/reform cause while an even larger crowd visited Court Square to listen to supporters of Williams.[11]

On election day both campaigns kept a close watch on the polls, looking for irregularities. Before the advent of voting machines, voters were handed a blank paper ballot when they entered their polling place. The voter then placed it in a locked ballot box after making a choice. Crump visited the fifth ward polling place and while there noticed an African American voter about to enter with a marked ballot. An argument ensued between the two. When the African American attempted to bypass Crump and enter the poll, the mayoral candidate hit him in the face. Crump then threatened further violence if he saw any more marked ballots.[12] When the polls closed and the votes were tabulated, the election commission announced that Crump had defeated Williams by a mere seventy-nine votes. "I shall attempt to carry out my pledges to the people, to give them an honest, efficient, and economical business government," the mayor-elect stated to the press. In contrast, Williams asserted that "the election has not been square and in all probability I will contest it."[13]

True to his word, Williams filed suit in chancery court the same day the election commission met to certify the results. The court refused to hear the case and Williams spent the next twelve months trying to convince a court to overturn the election.[14] Unwilling to have total faith in the courts, Williams also filed a petition with the legislative council alleging Crump and his allies stole the election and demanded the council investigate and rule on the validity of the contest.[15] The crux of Williams's petition was that several hundred new Memphians, who did not have the required six months of residency, had been allowed to vote. The disgruntled former mayor also claimed that at least 125 "phantom" citizens voted for his opponent, and that pro-Crump election officials failed to count at least fifty votes for him.[16] Williams had no documentation of actual fraud, but instead relied on friendly poll watchers for his information. Was the losing candidate right? Did the progressive mayor begin his term with a fraudulent election? It is impossible to know, but there is little doubt that both camps engaged in these questionable practices. Regardless of the truth, Williams's petition went nowhere. The legislative council passed a resolution stating it did not have the time to hear the case before the new commission took office, effectively ending Williams's case.[17]

At nine o'clock on the morning of January 1, 1910, George L. Harris, secretary of outgoing mayor James H. Malone, walked into city hall to watch the mayor-elect's inauguration and prepare a reception in his honor. To Harris's surprise, Mayor Crump was already sworn in and hard at work.[18] Crump wanted fast action on appointments to key city positions and did not have time for a party. The commission met for six hours, and appointed virtually every important city post, including city attorney, city court clerk, superintendent of the health department, and the chiefs of the fire and police departments.[19] The new form of government concentrated authority in the hands of five men who acted as both department heads and legislators; as one of these five officials, the mayor served as both city executive and head of the public affairs and health department. In order for the new mayor to achieve his progressive goals, he had only to convince two other commissioners to allow his will to prevail.

The first major ordinance of Crump's mayoralty was the creation of a civil service commission. Limited in scope, the commission dealt only with the hiring of police and fire department employees. Applicants were required to fill out a form to be eligible for employment, including certificates signed by six tax-paying citizens of Memphis who vouched for the applicant's good moral character. Examinations on reading, writing, arithmetic, and city geography were given to those with good moral character, and those with the highest scores were hired.[20] The testing of applicants may have been a step forward in eliminating political corruption, but not favoritism. The requirement that six citizens vouch for the prospective employee made it doubtful that anyone who was recommended by a political opponent of Crump was ever hired. Nor did the new civil service commission do anything about the larger practice of appointing political supporters to other city jobs.

The new mayor then attempted to distance his administration from the underworld when he asked citizens to report any allegations of graft against city employees. As a progressive, Crump was opposed to public employees profiting from their service. For instance, the mayor refused to accept a free pass from the Yazoo and Mississippi Valley Railroad Company and he expected others to follow his example.[21] When they did not, condemnation swiftly followed. Two months into the new administration, police chief Will Hayes attended a banquet hosted by notorious gangster John Persica, owner of the Garden Theater. During the course of the evening, Persica presented Chief Hayes with a solid gold badge set with seven diamonds. Concerned about the propriety of the gift, Crump ordered Hayes to return it.

When the mayor discovered that city employee George King was lending money to other workers he ordered the practice "stopped at once as no man can work for this government and be a party to such transactions."[22] Crump boasted that every "instance since this government came into power, whenever there was the slightest proof of graft, the offender has been promptly discharged."[23] In his second term, the commission adopted a resolution requiring each city department to offer a reward of fifty dollars for anyone who furnished "substantial proof that any individual connected with the city government has been guilty of so-called graft."[24] Along these same lines, Crump focused attention on the strict enforcement of city laws. Memphis police closed gaming establishments as well as many saloons. More police officers were put on the streets in 1910 and they made 3,467 more arrests than in the previous year.[25]

The biggest law enforcement issue in Tennessee was the state's prohibition on the sale and manufacture of liquor; enacted in 1909, the measure added a tremendous burden to local government. Although improving law enforcement was a priority of the new administration, prohibition was not. The reform element in Memphis was staunchly prohibitionist and they assumed Crump was sympathetic. When a committee of the Law Enforcement League visited the new mayor to discuss the issue, they were shocked when told he had no intention of enforcing the law. Crump explained that most Memphians did not want prohibition and he had other law enforcement priorities. The mayor stated that "the state is endeavoring to make Memphis enforce the law which the legislature passed over the protest of the majority of voters of the city."[26] Although disturbed by his opposition to prohibition, most reformers did not abandon the mayor because of his broader progressive agenda.[27] However, periodically the Anti-Saloon and Law Enforcement Leagues challenged Crump to "take a stand for law enforcement."[28]

Perhaps the most important tenet of Crump-style progressivism was the belief that government had the right to regulate utilities in order to make them more responsible to the people they served. The first to feel the pressure of government regulation in Memphis were the transportation utilities. The city commission passed an ordinance requiring headlights to be used by streetcars and railroad locomotives inside the city limits between the hours of sunset and sunrise. Noncompliance meant a fine of between five and fifty dollars.[29] The new government oversaw an agreement reached in December 1909 for the major railroads to build underpasses (called subways at the time, as the rails passed over the street) at eleven major intersections around the city. By the end of Crump's first term, underpasses at Carolina Street, as well as Lamar and Rayburn avenues, had been completed. One railroad attempted to back out of its contract but was forced to comply after the mayor informed them that if their agreement was not fulfilled, he would tear up any tracks crossing city streets.[30]

In addition to requiring the Memphis Street Railway Company to put headlights on its cars, Crump requested that service be increased to alleviate overcrowding.[31] Several new lines were added to the existing streetcar routes, including a crosstown line that connected the eastern portion of the city with the downtown business district. Despite the increase in service, Crump remained critical of the company. He often referred to the corporation as the "streetcar gang," and was never satisfied with its performance. In order to force the company to modernize, the commission awarded franchises to other streetcar companies to operate in portions of the city not yet covered by the Memphis Street Railway.[32] In response, the company upgraded its equipment, increased the number of cars in service, and added additional routes.

The utilities that garnered the most attention from city hall were the privately owned electric power companies. Two separate corporations provided electricity for the city; the Memphis Consolidated Gas and Electric Company provided power to residences while the Merchants Light and Power Company supplied local businesses. Crump viewed the dual system as a waste of resources and a primary reason that Memphians paid ten cents per kilowatt hour while their government spent $225,000 annually for lights.[33] Throughout his first term the mayor argued for a city-owned light plant despite opposition from the utilities and the *Memphis Commercial Appeal*. The public ownership of electrical service became the centerpiece of Crump's combative style of progressivism.

Regulation was not confined merely to utility companies during Crump's mayoralty. In 1911 the city commission took a small step towards regulating the labor of children when it passed an ordinance restricting the hours boys under the age of eighteen could work shining shoes and boots. Bootblack stands staffed by underage boys were required to close at seven o'clock in the evening during the week and at noon on Sundays and holidays.[34]

Public health was another area in which the role of government was expanded in Memphis. The noted physician Max Goltman was appointed head of the city's board of health, where he struggled to improve sanitary conditions in the Bluff City. One of Goltman's most important initiatives was the regulation of the milk industry.

He inspected several local dairies and ordered them to clean up their facilities and avoid milking cattle infected with bovine tuberculosis. Crump supported Goltman in his efforts, pushing through the commission an ordinance requiring all milk manufacturers to obtain an inspection permit before selling their wares in the city.[35] In order to prevent the spread of illness, the board of health was granted authority to examine children for communicable and contagious diseases during school hours, with teachers required to set aside time for examinations. Teachers were subject to arrest and fine if a child showing symptoms of a disease was allowed to return to school without a doctor's certificate.[36]

Similarly, midwives were required to take an examination and receive a license before they could practice their trade. Once licensed, they had to report any assistance provided to an expectant mother to local health authorities.[37] The commission took control of a privately owned tuberculosis hospital and also established a site for a communicable diseases facility.[38] Attempting to eradicate conditions that spread disease, the city building inspector also increased the number of condemnations, many on the personal recommendation of the mayor.[39]

Progressive regulations enacted during Crump's first term included a board of charity which disbursed city funds to the needy[40] and a board of censors which reviewed movies and plays in order to "exclude from public exhibition those not deemed fit for the people to see."[41] City funds were placed in a bank that paid 3.85 percent interest, which resulted in a profit of $14,000 for Memphis' coffers. The added revenue allowed the commission to lower the tax rate $1.59.[42] All of these efforts translated into strong political support from the white middle class as the 1911 city election season began.

The controversy surrounding the previous election convinced Crump it was imperative to build support within Shelby County's political machinery in order to prevent a recurrence of the events of 1909. The mayor was successful in placing two of his supporters on the Shelby County Democratic Executive Committee the year he first took office, which gave him influence over who was nominated in the local primary and ultimately who won in the general election. Along the same lines, in the election of 1910 Crump-supported Democrats filled Shelby County's eleven seats in the Tennessee General Assembly.[43] Nominal control of the Shelby County delegation to the legislature meant Crump was one of several recognized powers in the state. The mayor traded on his statewide influence to secure friendly appointments to the local election commission.[44] Thus men loyal to the mayor were charged with certifying election returns, including any that might be disputed. Leverage over state government was paramount for municipal leaders in Tennessee because the four major cities did not have home rule. Any authority not specifically given to a municipality by its charter had to be cleared by the general assembly.

Crump had strong support within the white middle class, but had paid little attention to the working class and African American communities before the 1911 municipal election. When he first entered politics, Crump had been an elitist who believed only the upper class should direct public affairs. But these views were abandoned as he learned to govern a diverse urban population. As mayor he had to consider the position of the working classes, ethnic groups such as Catholics and Jews, organized labor, and African Americans. Memphians were very politically active and they forced Crump to adapt to their demands. The political activities of these groups, particularly African Americans, had a profound effect upon the mayor. He abandoned the race baiting used in the 1909 campaign and adopted the theme of inclusion for his reelection bid. In a newspaper advertisement Crump promised to provide a city government that would be "for the benefit of the whole public, with no special favor to any."[45] And he was as good as his word. In 1915

African American pastor T. J. Searcy went to city hall to purchase a dog license and while there was ignored and otherwise treated in "a very uncouth and impolite way."[46] Angry at these slights, Searcy complained to Mayor Crump, who promptly replied: "It has always been the policy of this government . . . to treat everyone with uniform courtesy, regardless of their station or mission, and you were entitled to like treatment."[47] Crump's adoption of an inclusive view of politics was a sincere one, but it must also be pointed out that he longed for greater electoral success. At the end of his tenure as mayor Crump stated: "The political machine which I have relied upon and sought to maintain is not composed of any particular faction or class, but of the people of Memphis at large."[48]

The 1911 municipal election was the first test of Crump's new brand of politics. He was again opposed by J. J. Williams, who hoped to capitalize on Crump's apparent weakness in the working class and black neighborhoods. As the election season began, the black community, disappointed by Crump's first term, formed the Colored Citizens Association to increase voter registration and lobby for neighborhood improvements. Formed by African American leaders Bert M. Roddy, Robert Church, Jr., and Harry Pace, the association hoped to win concessions from the candidates in exchange for their support. The leadership met individually with both candidates and made it clear that certain priorities, such as street paving and a park reserved for African Americans, must be promised if they were to win the black vote.[49]

In an effort to expand his base, Crump stated that "the colored citizens of Memphis are undoubtedly entitled to park privileges." He then ordered the park commission to choose a suitable location for the city to purchase.[50] The Colored Citizens Association endorsed Crump, and in his second term the city opened Douglass Park for black use. Ignoring the fact that he had relied on the black vote in 1909, Williams charged that Crump's candidacy was a threat to white supremacy.[51] Ignoring Williams's racist charges, Crump appointed ward chairmen to oversee the campaign on the neighborhood level. The chairmen kept a tally of poll tax receipts, hung signs and banners on major streets, and collected campaign contributions.[52] The campaign compiled a list of voters who did not cast ballots in the previous election and sent each a letter urging them to vote.[53] The business community remained firmly with the mayor; many campaigned for him and contributed to his effort. In one instance a grocery store executive sent a circular to his managers requesting they vote for the Crump ticket.[54]

In addition, Crump worked closely with several grassroots organizations that formed in the early years of the twentieth century. As early as 1910, neighborhoods in Memphis established improvement associations to lobby for city services. As mayor, Crump worked closely with many of the civic organizations, including the City Club and the Lamar Park Improvement Club.[55] The City Club was formed in 1908 to "bring together frequently men who believe in the complete separation of party politics from the administration of all local political affairs."[56] The professionals, business leaders, and progressives who made up the organization involved themselves in many aspects of municipal affairs and often conducted investigations of city government.[57]

These efforts paid huge dividends for the mayor and his lieutenants; Crump carried every election precinct, with a total of 11,432 to 3,536 for Williams. The mayor's landslide reelection was not only a ringing endorsement of business progressivism, but was also a testament to the political prowess of the African American community in Memphis. The election insured that reform would continue for quite some time owing to a charter amendment which extended the mayor's term to four years. Soon after taking the mayoral oath for the second time, Crump took his first major steps onto the platform of statewide politics.

Tennessee Democrats had long been split over the issue of prohibition. In general, rural party members supported the measure, while their urban counterparts, like Crump, opposed it. Despite having signed prohibition into law, Governor Malcolm Patterson (1907–11) split the Democratic Party over this controversial measure when he vetoed a bill forbidding the sale of liquor near schools and with his pardon of the murderers of a prominent prohibitionist.[58] Antiliquor Democrats joined with prohibitionist Republicans in a "fusionist" ticket, and Republican Ben W. Hooper was elected governor in 1910.[59] Crump had remained neutral in 1910, but as 1912 began he hoped to unify Democrats and reclaim the governor's office for his party. In the spring Crump attempted to bring the two factions together in a "harmony" ticket headed by Congressman Kenneth McKellar, but the representative refused to run.[60] Democratic regulars supported former governor Benton McMillan (1899–1903), but Crump felt the former executive was not committed enough to progressive reform so he backed Chattanooga banker T. R. Preston.[61]

He soon regretted this decision because Preston was far from an energetic candidate. Frustrated by his lackadaisical attitude, Crump lashed out at Preston: "I am mightily afraid we are overlooking some of our very best bets; that is to say, the details are not being looked after. . . . [D]etails concerning a political fight are just as important as details concerning the banking business. . . ."[62] Crump's fears were realized on primary day when Preston received a mere 568 votes to McMillin's 512, even though there were 25, 000 registered voters in Shelby County.[63] It is difficult to determine what was responsible for the lack of ballots cast. The inactivity of Preston as well as the infighting within the Democratic Party certainly contributed to the situation. Crump felt the low voter turnout was due to an "awful steal" perpetuated by McMillan Democrats. Regardless of the reason, Shelby County's tepid support of Preston helped McMillin win the Democratic nomination in the rest of the state. Embarrassed by this turn and not convinced McMillin could beat Hooper, the mayor vowed to remain neutral in the fall contest.[64]

But he did not remain neutral for long. On the eve of the November election, Crump announced he would vote for the Democratic nominee.[65] The mayor unleashed his nascent electoral juggernaut, which contributed to McMillan winning Shelby County with 8,169 votes to Governor Hooper's 2,262.[66] However, this was not enough to offset Hooper's support in the rest of the state, which secured a second term for the Republican executive.[67] The results of the 1912 gubernatorial race suggested Crump was an important political leader, but it hardly translated into statewide power. However, he soon had another opportunity to secure political influence over Tennessee when controversy erupted over the collection of back taxes owed the state.

In early 1912, several Memphis business owners complained to the mayor that Tennessee comptroller Frank Dibrell was unfairly collecting back taxes from their establishments while ignoring commercial enterprises in Tennessee's rural counties.[68] In late January, Crump hired accountant Homer K. Jones to investigate the comptroller's records to "see why these fellows are so industrious in efforts to collect every dollar they can get."[69] Crump requested Dibrell turn over the available records, but the comptroller refused to do so.[70] Dibrell claimed the real reason Crump challenged him was that the mayor wanted the comptroller to stop collecting money from Memphis liquor dealers. Crump vowed to remove him from office if Dibrell would not comply. "I did not desire to be a party to such a nefarious deal, which would have perhaps guaranteed my election and cheated the state out of several thousand dollars," the comptroller reported to the press.[71]

Calling the mayor a tool of the liquor interests had become a common accusation of anti-Crump Tennesseans, so few who were not already inclined cared about the comptroller's allegation. In a letter made public by Dibrell, Crump ridiculed the comptroller's argument: "The people . . . are utterly indifferent as to whether I am as tricky as a trained mule, or you are as saintly as an angel. The public does want to know, however, what has become of the money collected by your office."[72] The mayor received many letters from across the state praising his demand for the comptroller to open his records,[73] but Dibrell remained adamantly opposed to cooperation with the "dishonorable" leader of Memphis.[74] In practical terms there was little Crump could do to force Dibrell to act other than bring public opinion to bear. However, Dibrell was vulnerable to Crump's machinations. The comptroller was elected by the general assembly, and Dibrell's term ended in 1913. Through his control of the Shelby delegation, Crump had the power to block Dibrell's election.

When the 1913 legislative session began, Crump traveled to Nashville, where he negotiated an alliance with the fusionists.[75] In exchange for their support of an investigative committee to look into the comptroller's operations, Crump agreed to lend the Shelby County delegation's votes to the fusionist's legislative agenda.[76] Faced with a potentially embarrassing investigation and a near certain defeat, Dibrell withdrew his candidacy and retired.[77] Crump's support of Benton McMillan and his deft crushing of Dibrell's political ambitions convinced many, most notably Governor Hooper, that Crump was not to be taken lightly as a statewide political force.

In the midst of his feud with Dibrell, the mayor also had to deal with one of the worst natural disasters in Memphis history. In the spring of 1912 the Mississippi River rose over forty feet, flooding parts of Memphis and the surrounding Mid-South. An estimated 1,500 refugees from the countryside poured into Memphis seeking food and shelter.[78] Governor Hooper provided tents for the homeless, while the city provided blankets and food. Resources available to local government were severely limited, so the mayor turned to U. S. Representative Kenneth McKellar and Senator Luke Lea. Crump asked McKellar to "have government send a quartermaster with funds to feed these people."[79] Federal assistance quickly arrived, including foodstuffs and $350,000 to shore up the broken North Memphis levee.[80] Not only did Crump secure federal money for flood damage; he also personally directed the rescue of several people stranded by high water.[81] Meanwhile, in Washington, McKellar and Lea met with President William Howard Taft to procure federal money for improvements to the levee system in and around Memphis.[82] Several times McKellar introduced legislation to provide the funds, but each time he failed.[83] Not until the New Deal would Crump secure a modern, effective flood control program for Memphis.

The pace of reform continued as the flood crisis ended. Expanding government regulation, the city commission enacted price controls through an ordinance that restricted the cost of phone service charged by the Cumberland Telephone Company. The price of a business line could not exceed $2.50 per month or $66 per year. Residential service could not exceed $2.50 a month for a private line or $2 a month for a party line.[84] In response, the phone company sued the city, and the U. S. Circuit Court of Appeals held that Memphis did not have the specific power to regulate phone rates. In 1913 the Shelby delegation introduced a bill giving Memphis the power to regulate prices, which passed the house and senate over considerable opposition from the telephone company.[85] Price controls were then extended to cab operators, who could not charge more than fifty cents for the first half mile of travel and ten cents for each additional one-fourth of a mile.[86] The commission also approved ordinances that restricted the pulling of trailers by trolley cars,[87] and required the Memphis Street Railway Company to maintain environmental controls in their trolleys. The average temperature was to be set at "no lower than fifty degrees Fahrenheit, nor when such car is heated by artificial heat, higher than seventy-five degrees Fahrenheit."[88]

Steps were taken to improve the attractiveness of the city as Crump became obsessed with Memphis's image. Property owners were required to keep their sidewalks free of debris,[89] while the commission also expanded an already existing law that regulated the installation of electrical wiring in buildings.[90] Public assistance was also increased during Mayor Crump's second term. In 1912 the board of charities, acting as an assistance clearinghouse, disbursed two thousand dollars to welfare organizations,[91] and the water company was required to provide their service free of charge to orphanages, senior citizens' homes, hospitals, and other charitable institutions.[92] Although these efforts were designed to improve the public welfare, there was another reason—Crump meticulously courted anyone whose support he needed for electoral victory, which meant he traded reform for votes.

The tax rate was lowered to shore up support from the business community, while Crump supported suffrage and built playgrounds to please women reformers. African Americans received increased, but still limited, access to city hall. For example, in 1914, a local theater scheduled a performance of Thomas Dixon's *The Leopard's Spots*, which contained racist portrayals of black characters. Learning of this, the Colored Men's Civic League met at St. John's Baptist Church and drafted a petition condemning the play as "calculated to inflame the feeling of some of our good white citizens in such a way as to widen the breach between the races" and requested the mayor forbid the performance.[93] A delegation of the membership met with Crump in his office where he listened patiently to their concern. The mayor turned the matter over to the board of censors, who promptly banned the play. In a statement to the press Crump explained: "I can see no good that a play of this character can do. Memphis has a very large negro [sic] population and a great majority of them are law abiding. The relations existing between the races here could not be better and

I seriously doubt the wisdom of permitting the production of any play that might be calculated to arouse any racial feeling."[94]

Prohibition remained the mayor's most significant problem. Local progressives remained opposed to Crump's position, while state officials were outraged by the lack of enforcement in Tennessee's largest city. Governor Ben Hooper promised to "clean out every saloon and every low-down dive in Memphis,"[95] but Crump's influence in the legislature blocked any potential action. Recognizing this, Hooper struck a deal with the Memphis leader in 1913. Crump pledged the Shelby delegation to the governor in exchange for Hooper's promise to exempt Memphis from prohibition enforcement.[96] This agreement had a direct impact on Crump's local reform program. A one-million-dollar bond issue had been introduced in the general assembly for the construction of a municipal light plant in Memphis; due to the mayor's alliance with Hooper, the bill passed. Citizens voted in favor of the bonds and the commission negotiated with the Merchants Power and Light Company, but talks broke down when a price could not be agreed upon.[97]

The governor however, was not true to his word. In October 1913, Hooper signed several law enforcement bills designed to coerce the municipalities into implementing prohibition. The centerpiece legislation was the Nuisance Act, which empowered local officials to close saloons, brothels, and gaming establishments by declaring them a public nuisance. The statute, however, did nothing to force recalcitrant officials to follow the law. The governor taunted the Memphis electorate: "You people wouldn't know majority rule if you were to meet it in the road. I say the liquor interests control your city."[98] Crump savagely responded by calling Hooper "a liar, a hypocrite, a thief, and an assassin."[99] As 1914 began, sentiment grew in Nashville for sterner measures to crush the defiance of antiprohibitionist officials, while local prohibitionists stepped up their criticism of the mayor.

Leading the fight was Shelby County attorney general Z. Newton Estes. The attorney general had worked closely with Crump,[100] but broke with him over prohibition. Openly critical of the mayor's lackadaisical enforcement of local laws, Estes tried to remove a Crump supporter from the county election commission. Referring to the mayor as "boss skunk tongue," Estes charged Crump with jury tampering in election fraud cases and accused him of planning the assassination of a detective working for the attorney general's office. Crump's response was just as unflattering: "Estes is nothing but . . . a common, vulgar-minded crook."[101] In order to challenge Estes's power in the county, Crump announced his candidacy for sheriff of Shelby County in the summer of 1914.[102] The mayor's goal in running for sheriff was "to break up some of the crooked work which has been going on with the full knowledge of Estes."[103]

The exchange of barbs made some uneasy over the direction of local government, but it was the arrogance displayed by Crump that led many to break with the mayor. From the perspective of the middle classes, the mayor should have resigned in order to run for sheriff. Holding both offices, they felt, was nothing more than a naked grab for power. *Memphis Commercial Appeal* editor C. P. J. Mooney argued: "Mr. Crump is the absolute master of all governmental affairs of Memphis" and if elected sheriff he "would have political power dangerous to the community—too great for any man to hold."[104] Even his loyalists were uneasy over this decision. Researching the municipal charter, city attorney Charles Bryan informed the mayor that Section 23 of the city charter prohibited city officials from holding any other city or county electoral office.[105] Not wanting to give up the mayoralty, Crump withdrew his candidacy for sheriff.

The mayor named John A. Reichman, head of associated charities and a member of the city's civil service commission, to run as the official Crump candidate. Reichman's candidacy, however, came too late. Judge Walter Malone ruled that Reichman's name could not appear on the ballot since he had failed to qualify by the specified time. Undaunted by the legal opinion, Crump organized his supporters in a write-in campaign. Concerned that the working classes would have trouble spelling Reichman on the write-in ballot, Crump loyalists held impromptu classes to teach voters how to spell the candidate's name.

Anti-Crump forces railed against what they perceived to be blatant electoral manipulation. The *Commercial Appeal* charged that the mayor was "seeking to teach a gin-drinking nigger enough to make a mark and write a name."[106] The white community paid little heed to these racist charges. Reichman won the write-in campaign by a heavy majority, which further expanded Crump's involvement in county government. In addition to his success in controlling the outcome of the county elections, Crump also played an important role in the 1914 Tennessee gubernatorial campaign.

As the campaign season began, antiprohibitionist Democrats abandoned their opposition to state law in hopes of wresting the governor's office from the Republicans. In May 1914 the party chose as their nominee a staunch prohibitionist, Henry County attorney general Thomas C. Rye. The nomination of Rye eliminated any reason for traditional Democrats to support Governor Hooper for a third term.[107] Anxious to see the party come together as it had not done in 1912, Crump enthusiastically supported Rye.[108] On election day, Shelby County Democrats cast fourteen thousand votes for Rye in contrast to Hooper's two thousand, which contributed to the Democratic nominee receiving 53 percent of the vote.[109] While hardly decisive, the vote in Shelby County was important and contributed to Crump's growing prestige. Democrats from across the state praised Crump for his strong support for Rye,[110] but their gratitude did not last long.

Memphis prohibitionists continued to step up their attacks on the mayor. Attorney General Estes sent a broadside to newspaper editors and state legislators depicting "the insurrection against law and order conducted by the Mayor of Memphis in his efforts to nullify the prohibition law."[111] The attorney general's machinations emboldened the rural/prohibitionist bloc to take further steps in curbing the power of Tennessee's municipalities. Responding to the call of Governor Rye, the legislature passed the Elkins Ouster Law in January 1915. The new statute provided a mechanism whereby the state could remove a public official from his position for neglecting his duties.[112] In a calculated move, Crump closed all saloons in Memphis the day after Governor Rye signed the ouster bill. Rye was content with this and expressed the opinion that "Estes dare not make any move against any official so long as the official was trying to do what was right."[113] The local progressive bloc was equally satisfied, electing Crump to a third term as mayor in April to begin in January 1916. But in August rumors reached the governor that Memphis saloons were again open.[114]

Reported collusion between the police and saloon owners convinced many in Memphis and Nashville that Crump either would not, or could not, enforce the law. An ouster petition was filed in September 1915, claiming the mayor was derelict in upholding prohibition and guilty of graft. Crump was not the only target; the removal of fire and police commissioner R. A. Utley and police inspector Oliver Perry were also demanded.[115] An audit found no financial irregularities and the ouster suit was dismissed.

Concerned that the liquor trade was back in business, Rye sent state attorney general Frank M. Thompson to investigate the Crump administration. According to a surveillance report passed to the mayor, Thompson met with the ouster petition signers and undoubtedly collected evidence from them.[116] Thompson filed a second ouster suit which repeated the prohibition charge but did not mention the graft accusation. As a result of the investigation, the list of defendants was augmented to include Sheriff Reichman and city judge W. M. Stanton. Crump and his codefendants pled not guilty in chancery court on October 20, but at the November 3 hearing the mayor, Utley, Stanton, and Perry reversed their stance and pled guilty. Sheriff Reichman maintained he was innocent and announced he would wait for trial. Chancery court then removed the four men from office, leaving Commissioner George C. Love as acting mayor.[117]

Crump appealed to the Tennessee Supreme Court, hoping the court would settle the issue of whether his removal was for his term which was about to end or included his third term, slated to begin in January 1916.[118] An injunction was issued preventing Crump from taking office while they deliberated. On February 12, 1916, the court ruled that Crump was guilty and upheld the chancery court's ouster. Settling the issue of the third term, the justices interpreted the law as being retroactive, which meant the evidence collected for the first suit could be used again. The probability was that he would be ousted a second time, so Crump took the oath of office, collected his back pay and then immediately resigned.[119] As might be expected, the now former mayor was outraged by this turn of events and he lashed out at those he thought responsible: "The corporate interests of Memphis have said that I have played too much politics while I was in office. That could have been expected in the light of the fact I have never allowed them or their attorneys to control me. . . ."[120]

The local media was quick to sound the death knell to Crump's political career. C. P. J. Mooney of the *Commercial Appeal* wrote: "On Washington's Birthday, when the souls of Americans should be filled with sentiments of unselfish patriotism, we saw in the city hall yesterday an exhibition of machine government at its worst. It was the ending of a chapter in a story of rotten politics, mal-administration and the rule of men who have no grasp of their duties as officials and citizens."[121]

A chapter in local politics may have ended in February 1916, but it remained to be seen whether E. H. Crump's public career had been permanently derailed.

"The Black Flag of Machine Politics"

Infuriated at being removed from office, the former mayor plotted his revenge. Even though his political career was in tatters, he still had the support of some in the business community,[1] and, more importantly, he still commanded the loyalty of the Shelby County delegation and his allies sat on the local election board. At the same time, Crump had developed in his mind a kind of master plan for Memphis which included flood control, publicly owned electrical service, and the end of statewide prohibition. Unfinished business related to these three issues was a major reason for Crump to stay in politics. With his base of support, Crump looked to the next election to reestablish his political supremacy. In the summer of 1916 Crump announced a slate of candidates for every major county office, including trustee, sheriff, and tax assessor. The trustee's slot was reserved for Crump, who was unwilling to remain behind the scenes. County trustees were allowed to pocket a portion of fees collected in lieu of a salary. This money could be very helpful in funding political campaigns and was no doubt a reason Crump sought the position.

Crump's opponent in the trustee's race was local attorney Harry Litty, who campaigned on the promise of ending the fee-sharing practice.[2] The former mayor refused to comment on the fee issue,

25

given that this was a major reason he sought the office. Litty was strongly supported by the *Commercial Appeal*, which attacked the ascent of the Crump political machine from every possible angle. Crump's mayoral administration was described as fostering "greed, extravagance, waste, and incompetency,"[3] and the "spirit of the Crump campaign is beer, booze and fees."[4] The Crump forces left little to chance. Political rallies were held throughout the county, and campaign workers took steps to insure that sympathetic voters were registered. Firefighters and police officials loyal to Crump ignored their duties and transported citizens to election commission offices for registration.[5] These efforts resulted in twenty-five thousand people, five thousand of whom were African American, becoming registered to vote in the August election.[6] The techniques employed by the machine increased the number of registered voters, but it also raised suspicions among the staff of the Litty campaign.

A house-by-house survey was done by Litty supporters and then compared to the voter registration books. According to affidavits collected by Litty's campaign manager, 2,900 people listed in the books could not be found residing anywhere in Memphis.[7] The election commission accepted the conclusions of the Litty forces but could do nothing to change the situation. State law prevented county election boards from purging allegedly fraudulent voters from their books. Their only option was to advise poll workers to prevent anyone from voting who could not prove they resided in Shelby County.[8]

As the campaign wore on, it became an increasingly bitter affair. Crump accused his opponent of being a stooge of the private utilities, while the *Commercial Appeal* gleefully reported attacks made by Litty: "Another broadside was fired into the piratical ship Crump, flying the black flag of machine politics. . . ."[9] Angry words led to violence when a fistfight erupted between Crump and Litty operatives.[10] By this time Crump was a desperate man. The ouster had affected him deeply, making him ruthlessly determined not to lose again. From Crump's perspective his back was against the wall and he was willing to do anything to regain political power. Gangster and Crump supporter Mike Haggerty, aided by sympathetic police officers, drove Litty supporters from a Beale Avenue polling place after they objected to 265 fraudulent votes being cast. Registrars loyal to Crump certified the ballots despite evidence of fraud.[11] Crump defeated Litty by over 2,000 votes,[12] roughly the same number of fraudulent registrations uncovered by the opposition. Tactics such as those employed on Beale Avenue gave county trustee Crump the dominance he craved and were instrumental in the creation of a powerful political machine. The 1916 election also further convinced middle-class Memphians that the newly elected county trustee was a dangerous politician.

Meanwhile, in the city, acting mayor Love resigned in February and was replaced by Thomas C. Ashcroft, commissioner of streets, bridges, and sewers.[13] Ashcroft swore allegiance to the deposed leader when he declared: "[S]o long as I occupy the mayor's office I shall consider [Crump] . . . the real mayor of Memphis."[14] Several Crump-appointed city officials were removed by Ashcroft, suggesting he had second thoughts about who was in charge. Angered by this betrayal, Crump began ouster proceedings against Ashcroft, which led to his resignation.[15] Harry Litty was appointed mayor in August 1917,[16] to serve until a special election was held. The appointment of Crump's former rival further marginalized him from city hall, but he remained committed to controlling the direction of municipal affairs.

The first opportunity for Crump to seize the reins of city government came in the special election of 1918. Mayor Litty declined to run, which left the field wide open. Former Shelby County sheriff Frank Monteverde was chosen to head Crump's machine ticket along with Crump, who sought a second term as trustee. In a move designed to enhance the former sheriff's credibility, Crump loyalists on the city commission removed Commissioner George Blackwell from the city commission and appointed Monteverde to the vacancy.[17] Anti-Crump Democrats, determined to crush the trustee's hold on the party, introduced a rival slate of candidates headed by George A. Macon, president of Macon and Andrews Business College. The machine had the upper hand going into the race because of its domination of the election commission, which meant the majority of workers assigned to polling places were loyal to Trustee Crump.[18] Macon's chances were further crippled by the continuing alliance between organization forces and noted black Republican Robert Church, Jr. Under the aegis of his Lincoln League, Church increased black voter registration much as the Colored Citizens Association had done in 1911.[19]

Control of the election commission and the support of African American voters assured a Crump victory. Monteverde received 3,665 ballots to Macon's 1,576, while Crump prevailed over his opponent by a 3,000-vote margin.[20] Despite the votes cast, there remained within the Memphis electorate a deep suspicion of the county organization. Many citizens viewed the factional nature of local politics as deplorable. Believing the city needed a new form of government, business leaders and middle-class progressives formed the Citizen's Committee of 100 under the direction of drug company executive Robert R. Ellis. Committee members believed the hiring of a city manager would eliminate factional squabbling and change the disquieting direction of local government. In July 1918 Ellis and others conferred with the Shelby County Democratic Executive Committee and requested their support for a change in the city charter. All candidates nominated by the Democratic Party pledged to vote for the appointment of a city manager who would "have exclusive charge of the affairs of the city."[21]

When the general assembly convened in early 1919, a bill was introduced in the Tennessee legislature to adopt the city manager plan for Memphis.[22] Despite the widespread support for the bill, not everyone believed it was a step forward. Several local politicians, most notably Mayor Monteverde, argued that the citizens of Memphis should be given the right to vote on the proposed changes to their government charter. No doubt Monteverde and the others were more concerned with their political futures than with advancing direct democracy. Regardless of the motive, their argument resonated with many voters. At a mass meeting held at the Lyric Theater in March, the mayor, city commissioners A. D. Mason and Dan Wolf, and former state supreme court justice A. S. Buchanan called the proposed charter "autocratic and opposed to the principles of a democratic government." A resolution was approved by the two thousand attendees requesting the legislature "refuse to pass the city manager bill" until a referendum provision was included.[23]

Sensing defeat, the Citizen's Committee of 100 sought out Crump in hopes his influence could sway members of the legislature. But it had the opposite effect. Some legislators saw the county trustee's involvement as a callous move to regain his lost dominion over Memphis. Nashville attorney Hill McAlister reported to Crump: "I have also heard it suggested . . . that the primary object of your new bill is to get out from under the affect of the ouster law and have a wide-open town."[24] Undaunted by these sentiments, Crump and the Citizen's Committee of 100 continued to push for the bill's passage. Shelby County representative Carl Larsen lobbied fellow legislators to vote for the bill,[25] while the trustee wrote to prominent Tennesseans seeking their endorsement.[26]

When Crump traveled to Nashville to lobby personally for the bill's passage, *Commercial Appeal* reporter Robert S. Hildebrand described the scene: "Edward H. Crump, deposed and discredited leader of the one-time powerful political machine in Shelby County today stood shorn of the last bit of wool he has attempted to pull over the eyes of the people of Memphis on the city manager bill. Without camouflage, Crump appeared in person at the capital today to lobby for his pet measure by which he hopes to return to power."[27] The specter of Crump as Memphis city manager haunted the corridors of the Tennessee General Assembly, while railroad workers and businessmen telegraphed members to abandon the measure.[28] The proposal did have some support but it had little effect on the deliberations in the capitol. Indeed, Crump made little headway with his own delegation.

Organization stalwart John Galella deserted his patron to lead opposition forces in the house,[29] and the rest of the Shelby County legislators soon followed. After four months of rancorous debate, the Tennessee House of Representatives defeated the measure forty-three to twenty-nine.[30] The decision of the legislature was a crushing blow to the trustee's prestige and revealed the weakness of his political organization. In many ways Crump had never been less popular than he was in the spring of 1919. True, he still controlled the machinery of government, but given the relative lack of power vested in Shelby County, there was little to control.

In addition to weakening Crump's position in Memphis, the city manager debacle also further alienated the middle class who yearned to eliminate factionalism from municipal government. Grassroots activists—business and professional men, suffragettes, and progressives—formed a nonaligned political organization called the Citizen's League to challenge the "juggernaut of graft and sinister politics."[31] At a mass meeting in August, a slate of candidates, headed by wholesale grocer Rowlett Paine, was chosen.[32] The county machine, still reeling from the city manager fight, sought to recapture the mayor's seat when it nominated county commissioner William J. Bacon for the post. Anti-Crump Democrats also joined the fray by once again nominating J. J. Williams.

The machine ticket failed to excite interest and unraveled when Bacon withdrew from the race in October. In an attempt to obscure how crippled they were, the organization leadership announced the day before the election their support of Paine.[33] The Citizen's League slate prevailed over Williams by 2,700 votes, which made it appear that the county organization was instrumental in Paine's victory. It is doubtful, however, that their involvement had any significant impact on the outcome when we consider how controversial the machine was in 1919.

In reality Rowlett Paine was elected mayor because of voter dissatisfaction with factional politics that E. H. Crump had come to represent. But this is not to suggest that Crump was politically impotent. In August of 1920 the county trustee was reelected to a third term, and the Shelby delegation, which remained under Crump's nominal control, played a crucial role in Tennessee's adoption of the women's suffrage amendment.[34] Despite these successes, the power exercised by Crump and his political organization was circumscribed. Indeed, two years later the trustee's position as the preeminent political leader in Shelby County was directly threatened during the gubernatorial election.

In 1922 Tennessee Democrats lusted for vindication after their defeat in the gubernatorial election of 1920. Republican Alfred A. Taylor defeated Governor Albert H. Roberts in part because of conservative anger over the Nineteenth Amendment.[35] Middle Tennessee attorney Austin Peay emerged victorious in the August primary without the support of the county machine. Crump again supported former governor Benton McMillan, but he lavished more attention on the county and other state elections. In May, the Shelby County Democratic Executive Committee endorsed Crump's ally Senator Kenneth McKellar for reelection over the objections of anti-Crump Democrats who favored the candidacy of attorney Guston Fitzhugh. Several Fitzhugh supporters resigned in the wake of the committee's actions, which no doubt pleased the Crump forces.[36]

Fitzhugh was perhaps the leading antimachine Democrat because he was a driving force during the ouster proceedings in 1915 that had done so much to alter Crump's political fortunes. Calling themselves independents, the anti-Crump forces challenged machine candidates in several county races, including that of trustee.[37] The City Club resurrected the controversy surrounding the splitting of fees between trustee and county when it demanded to know if Crump would attack the constitutionality of a newly enacted state law that abolished the fee system. Crump responded that he supported ending the fee-sharing practice as long as the monies remained "in Shelby County rather than be sent to Nashville and distributed over the state. . . ."[38]

Crump's forceful response to the City Club revealed his views on the county's relationship with the rest of Tennessee. It was felt by Crump that Shelby County paid more taxes owing to its large population and thus should receive state funds commensurate with its size. The county leader hoped to unify the Democratic Party under his leadership in order to dictate terms regarding the dispersal of state funds to the gubernatorial nominee. The first step in that unification came at a mass meeting in June, where seven hundred machine Democrats elected officers to direct the campaign.[39] Although Crump and his ablest lieutenant Frank Rice were not in attendance they almost certainly directed the affair from behind the scenes. Chairman T. K. Riddick, vice chairman Mrs. Lee Mallory, and the other officers created a "committee of 21" to slate candidates for the general assembly.

The members of the committee were a cross section of the white electorate, and were a microcosm of the county machine. Included in its ranks were six women, three labor union representatives, and several farmers, bankers, men with small businesses, and veterans.[40] The slate of candidates chosen by the committee had representatives from labor and the business and professional classes, and included Marion Griffin, the first woman attorney in Tennessee.[41] In addition to unifying the local party, the organization leadership continued to focus attention on voter participation. During the July supplemental registration, the number of voters was augmented by fifteen thousand, leading to a total of thirty-five thousand registered voters in Shelby County.[42] In the August county election all candidates chosen by the committee won, including Crump, who was reelected to a fourth trustee term. At the same time Kenneth McKellar defeated Guston Fitzhugh by eight thousand votes in the senatorial primary, and, as already stated, Austin Peay won the party's gubernatorial primary.[43] Anti-Crump Democrats had faltered badly in their bid to unhinge the trustee's grip on Shelby County. As one independent described the situation, "[I]t was just a case of too much organization."[44]

Given his success in the August elections, Crump expected the gubernatorial nominee to humbly come and trade for the county leader's support. Peay, however, apparently presumed that as the nominee he would automatically receive the support of Shelby County Democrats. Local Republicans noticed the lack of enthusiasm for Peay and expanded the campaign for their nominee, Alf Taylor. Alarmed by the gathering strength of the GOP, state Democratic chairman Joseph W. Byrns telephoned Crump in late October to learn why there was no active Peay campaign in Shelby County. In a statement to the press Crump reported that he "suggested that in order to arouse enthusiasm it would be both wise and fair for Mr. Peay to advocate repeal of the public utilities law, and . . . a fair division of the automobile license tax."[45]

With Crump's demands laid on the table, McKellar hoped to bring the two camps together. A meeting was arranged for Sunday, October 29, but each side refused to meet with the other. Instead, Crump traveled to Holly Springs to visit his mother, while Peay met with grocery store magnate Clarence Saunders, whom he named his Memphis campaign manager.[46] Saunders was as much a colorful personality as Crump and had made millions with his self-service Piggly Wiggly groceries. A key ingredient in Saunders's success was the use of publicity to promote his wares, and he brought all his skills to bear in selling Austin Peay to the Memphis electorate. At a rally in Gaston Park a musical band and fireworks were employed,[47] while full-page ads were placed in the newspapers which excoriated Crump as much as they extolled Peay:

> Free Men! Free Women!
> Who is Master? Who the Servant?
> Blowing fire and prophesying destruction to all who may oppose him, the Political Boss, drunk with the power of subdued wills of trembling men who fear him, he even has the "gall" to tell our next Governor of Tennessee that unless you take my bidding and surrender your will, I will see that you are not the next Governor of Tennessee. And what did Austin Peay do? He refused to submit to such dictation— he refused to be a coward—he refused to wear the collar of the Political Boss.[48]

Not to be outdone, Crump offered a justification for his position:

> MEMPHIS AND SHELBY COUNTY
> WANT A SQUARE DEAL
> I am more interested in Memphis and Shelby County than I am in any man or set of men in Tennessee politics.
> Shelby County is not getting a fair and square deal. This county has Paid into the state treasury $812,625.97 in automobile taxes, and has Received in return $21,257.83 . . . Am I to be censured because I have endeavored to assist the people of Memphis and Shelby County? . . .[49]

Peay remained unwilling to meet his demands, so Crump swallowed his Democratic pride and turned to Republican nominee Taylor. The exact details of their agreement is unknown, but when Taylor announced on election eve that he supported a more equitable distribution of the automobile tax and the repeal of the public utilities law, it was clear that an accommodation had been reached.[50] This was confirmed on election day, when organization leaders sported buttons that declared they were "Taylor Democrats."[51]

Between these warring factions sat McKellar. As a politician who depended on the votes of Democrats from across Tennessee, the senator naturally did not want to break with the party. On the other hand, he felt personally loyal to Crump and hated to turn against his old friend. On election eve McKellar arrived in Memphis with the gubernatorial nominee to attend a final rally and closely monitor the next day's proceedings. The senator drove to the rally with Peay in an automobile owned by Clarence Saunders. In his speech to the three-thousand-plus audience McKellar dispelled any doubts about his loyalty: "Some of my best friends are members of the county Democratic organization. Mayor Crump has always been my friend and he is my friend now. I would not be fair to you or to myself if I did not acknowledge that friendship."[52] The results of the election were a mixed bag for the machine. Peay won Shelby County by a two-thousand-vote majority, but the organization's legislative ticket was easily elected.[53] Crump and his lieutenants therefore could not directly control the governor, but with a solid block of delegates to the general assembly they had the power to thwart Peay's legislative program.

When the legislature convened in early 1923, the two Democratic factions lined up to do battle. The first skirmish came when the Shelby delegation introduced a bill to abolish the charter of the tiny hamlet of Eads. At first glance this seemed to be nothing more than a routine matter; the bill's sponsors claimed Eads's population was too small to sustain a township. But there was another reason. Withdrawing the charter would strip Eads of its representation on the county court, which was held by an anti-Crump Democrat.[54] The purpose of the Eads bill was thus to retaliate against a recalcitrant county official while at the same time reminding the governor who really controlled Shelby County. Governor Peay was not impressed. He promptly vetoed the measure, declaring: "I cannot countenance a move so palpably political as the Eads bill."[55] Correctly interpreting this as a threat to their hegemony, Crump lieutenant Frank

Rice rallied the organization faithful in the senate, who overrode the veto by a vote of eighteen to five. The measure was then introduced in the house, where Crump stalwart Lois Bejach pleaded with his colleagues to reject the governor's action because "Eads is only a crossroads. Not a cent has ever been spent there for municipal purposes."[56] Bejach's argument failed to sway house members, who sustained Peay's veto by fifty-six votes.[57] Emboldened by his victory, the governor laid plans to destroy the county trustee's political organization.

The second great battle in this legislative war between county trustee and governor came when the term ended for the state election commissioner for West Tennessee; held by Crump loyalist John C. Carey, the appointment ended on April 1, 1923. Instead of reappointing Carey, the legislature followed Governor Peay's lead and tapped Obion County senator Sam Bratton to fill the seat. The state election commission was made up of two Democrats and one Republican from Tennessee's three grand divisions. Election commissioners appointed the county election boards and certified state election returns, giving them considerable influence over local affairs.[58] To further circumvent Crump's power, the governor introduced a bill that would expand the number of election commissioners from three to five.[59] In practical terms this would have given the governor of Tennessee nearly absolute control over the state's election machinery.

This was too much for some legislators, even those who staunchly supported Governor Peay. One senator exclaimed: "It is factional politics, inspired by one faction to gain advantage over the other. . . ."[60] The bill passed in the house, yet stalled in the senate. For eight hours anti-Peay forces filibustered the measure, refusing to let it come up for a vote. When a vote was finally taken, all the administration could muster was a simple majority, which was not enough to secure passage.[61] The governor was further humiliated when former election commissioner Carey sued the state, claiming the constitution did not allow his successor to serve as both state senator and election commissioner. The court upheld Carey's argument and reinstated him to the election commission.[62]

When the general assembly adjourned in April, the Crump and Peay forces had fought each other to a standstill. The governor had won a marginal victory in successfully vetoing the Eads bill, but failed miserably in his attempt to gain control of the state election commission. Despite their success in maintaining influence over the state election machinery, Crump and his lieutenants were foiled in punishing a county official perceived to be disloyal. The stalemate forced Austin Peay to reevaluate his commitment to destroying Crump's political base, while the county trustee looked to the fall municipal election to restore his fortunes in Memphis.

The relationship between Crump and Mayor Rowlett Paine had never been a close one, but the two were hardly enemies. Early in Paine's term they had squabbled over the mayor's failure to increase the pay of African American schoolteachers and Paine's removal of a Crump stalwart from the park commission. But these were minor affairs. Both men shared the political values of the progressive movement. During Paine's first term of office he increased taxes allocated for local schools, appointed Camille Kelly to the juvenile court bench, adopted a zoning ordinance that restricted commercial development in residential neighborhoods, and created a city planning commission.[63] From Crump's perspective the problem with Paine was not in his policies but rather his lack of allegiance.

As the campaign approached, Crump compiled a list of Paine's weaknesses, such as "do not cut weeds, which are lapping over sidewalks all over city ... very scarce garbage collection during the summer."[64] Hoping to exploit these issues, the trustee met with his lieutenants to plan election strategy in early September.[65] The details of this meeting are unclear, but on October 5 the *News-Scimitar* newspaper reported that "authentic circles" assured them the county machine would support a ticket headed by bank president Charles W. Thompson.[66] The next day however, Thompson announced he would not run.[67] It is not known what happened, but this ended Crump's hopes of affecting the mayoral race, at least publicly. The aborted Crump slate included city judge Lewis Fitzhugh, who was not seeking another term. When the ticket collapsed, Fitzhugh announced he was running for mayor, which suggests the possibility that Crump had a hand in the decision.

The overriding issue of the 1923 city election, however, was not Crump's machinations or the accomplishments of Mayor Paine. Rather it was the growing influence of the Ku Klux Klan. Founded in 1921, the Memphis chapter, or klavern, was estimated to have ten thousand members by 1923.[68] The potential impact of the Klan on local affairs was not lost on the political establishment. Mayor Paine hesitated to alienate this potential bloc of votes, especially when it was rumored they would support him in the upcoming election.[69] As Memphians debated the possible relationship between city hall and the secret empire, a feud erupted between Paine and his secretary, Clifford Davis, over the latter's candidacy for city judge. Paine objected to this, and when Davis refused to withdraw from the race the mayor dismissed him.[70] Faced with the loss of Paine's political support, Davis turned to the Klan. When the Memphis klavern announced their slate of candidates for the municipal election, Davis was their choice for city judge.[71]

Davis's relationship with the Klan put Paine in an awkward position, and he moved quickly to extricate himself from the charge that he was pro-Klan. Paine denounced the Klan vociferously, and they responded in kind.[72] There was a strong base of anti-Klan sentiment in Memphis led by the *Commercial Appeal*, which was awarded the Pulitzer Prize in 1923 for savagely attacking the invisible empire of the Klan.[73] Not surprisingly, African Americans comprised an important part of this coalition. Laughably the Memphis Klavern held a rally on Beale Avenue where they urged the two hundred black attendees to join them because "both were native born Americans and both were protestant."[74] African American voters were naturally unimpressed with this argument. Several black leaders, including Colored Citizens Association founder Bert Roddy, Solvent Savings Bank president T. H. Hayes, drugstore owner J. B. Martin, and Republican George W. Lee declared in a public statement: "The colored voters of Memphis are supporting the Paine administration ticket straight. . . . We believe that they will give us a square deal. . . . We want every colored man and woman to vote the ticket."[75] Several rallies were held for black voters, including one at the Venus Theater, where noted black Republican Roscoe Conkling Simmons urged them to vote.[76] With the black vote squarely in Paine's column, the question became who would the county machine support?

It certainly was not going to be the Klan. In many ways the invisible empire was the antithesis of Crump's political organization. While the Klan believed strongly in excluding all who were different, especially blacks, Catholics, and Jews, Crump believed strongly in inclusion. That is not to say all were equal. African American political participation did not lead to black officeholders, while women remained at the margins of the decision-making process. However, within those strictures, there was an opportunity to participate.

Many political observers were convinced Crump was silently backing Fitzhugh. Seemingly this was confirmed when an anonymous full-page advertisement appeared in the *Commercial Appeal*. Written in the Crump style, the ad rhetorically asked voters: "Will You Vote for Hypocrisy and Paine or for Judge Fitzhugh and Anti-Klan?"[77] On October 31, however, Crump declared: "I have had nothing whatever to do with either the Fitzhugh or the Paine Tickets. . . ."[78] This may or may not have been true, but the day before the election he signaled his support for Paine when Frank Rice and several other machine stalwarts suddenly appeared at Paine campaign headquarters and quietly went to work.[79]

The support engendered by Crump's last-minute decision no doubt played a part in Paine's subsequent electoral victory, but it was not decisive. Mayor Paine received twelve thousand votes to the Klan's seven thousand, while Fitzhugh polled slightly less than three thousand ballots. Most of Paine's support came from the white middle-class suburbs and the black downtown wards.[80] Given the unwavering support of the white middle class for the mayor, it is easy to conclude that African American voters, rather than the county machine, played the decisive role in Paine's reelection.

Since 1915 E. H. Crump had sought to wipe away the stain of political disgrace engendered by his ouster from city hall. He had partly achieved this through his election to the county trustee's post and the construction of an efficient political organization in Shelby County. However, he was hamstrung in his goal of returning to power in Memphis by the popularity of Governor Austin Peay and Mayor Rowlett Paine. The emergence of a politically influential Ku Klux Klan in Memphis further restricted Crump's movement and threatened to shatter his carefully built coalition. As 1924 began, all-out war loomed between the machine, Governor Peay, and the Klan.

"The People Have Made Their Statement"

Crump hoped to stem the power of the Klan and Governor Peay by expanding his influence beyond the borders of Tennessee. His first step in this plan was to attend the 1924 Democratic National Convention in New York. Although by no means a national figure, Crump was not unknown in national political circles. In 1916 for example, President Woodrow Wilson extended New Year's greetings to the former mayor.[1]

In order to secure a position at the convention, Crump needed the support of Democratic leaders from around the state. Acting on the trustee's behalf, Senator Kenneth McKellar canvassed fellow Democrats to determine the level of support for Crump's candidacy for a position as delegate. Unfortunately, some of the replies were not encouraging. "I am sorry that I cannot consistently speak favorably of your friend Crump.... [Y]ou had better persuade the Republicans to give Crump some sort of reward and get him off your list," reported one Tennessee Democrat.[2]

Not all Democrats were so harsh. Writing to Crump, Knoxville bank president William S. Shields declared: "I hear that you want to go to the National Democratic convention as a delegate from the state at large.... I take pleasure in telling you that I will support you cordially in East Tennessee and I think I can render you some

41

valuable service."[3] Frank Rice investigated political conditions in Nashville,[4] and Crump traveled to Fayette County to secure its support.[5] Crump was chosen as an at-large delegate during a state convention in Nashville.[6] Those who attended the state meeting were chosen by the secretary of the credentials committee, who carried out the wishes of the Shelby organization. A friendly secretary no doubt ensured Crump's selection and kept the Klan from dominating the proceedings.[7]

Traveling to New York in June, Crump supported Woodrow Wilson's son-in-law William G. McAdoo for the Democratic Party's presidential nomination.[8] When McAdoo was unable to carry the day, Crump voted for John W. Davis as the party's presidential choice despite private misgivings about Davis's chances.[9] During the convention he listened intently to Franklin Roosevelt nominate New York governor Alfred E. Smith and was impressed with his acumen.[10] More importantly, Crump watched with disgust as representatives of the Klan tried to dominate the convention.[11] Writing Massachusetts senator David I. Walsh, the trustee predicted that "such an un-American and bitter organization as the Ku Klx Klan is bound to perish from the earth."[12]

Along with the Klan, another potential threat to the county machine was the administration of Governor Austin Peay. As already stated, the governor and Crump had fought each other to a standstill in 1923. Both men probably wanted to reach an accommodation, but Peay was the first to move when he sent an emissary to Senator McKellar offering a deal. The governor promised to secure Crump a seat at the convention in exchange for future support. As McKellar rightly pointed out in a letter to Crump, the governor's support was not needed.[13] However, the trustee was amenable to an understanding. Peay agreed to establish a medical school in Memphis and endorse Crump's choice for state election commissioner in exchange for supporting the governor's reelection bid.[14]

As the 1924 campaign season began, Crump announced he was not going to seek another term as trustee. Despite his stepping down, Crump remained the head of the machine and was elected a member of the state Democratic committee.[15] The county organization took steps in January 1924 to eliminate the Klan threat by blocking the invisible empire's attempt to elect a sympathetic chairman of the Shelby County Quarterly Court.[16] The final assault against the secret empire was launched in the summer when the organization named a full slate of candidates to counter the Klan, who boasted they would seize control of the county by winning the August election. Crump was, of course, determined to prevent a Klan victory.[17] Two things were in the organization's favor. First, the possibility of a bitter primary fight was eliminated when the governor and Crump reached their understanding. Secondly, the alliance between the machine and city hall continued as Mayor Paine endorsed the Crump ticket.[18]

The Klan tried their best to garner the vote in the white working-class neighborhoods of South Memphis and Binghampton, but they were unable to overcome the continued marriage between the black downtown wards and the white middle class. All of the organization's candidates won handily, while Austin Peay received a fifteen-thousand-vote majority over his opponents in the primary.[19] The Klan had been crushed politically, but elements of the secret order hoped an opportunity would arise in the future to pay Crump back for their humiliating defeats. The county leader reciprocated their hatred. In a letter to an old friend, Crump wrote: "We are all most 'hap-ee' over the election, in which we defeated the Ku Klux over two to one. I almost lose my equilibrium when the Ku Klux are being discussed. Were I . . . a genius in the use of epithets, words would still have no power to express my contempt for these anonymous slanderers."[20]

The rapprochement between Crump and Peay satisfied both factions in the short term, but neither was totally comfortable with the situation. Conditions were exacerbated when Crump learned from the governor's secretary that Peay was considering a run for a third term.[21] Traditionally Tennessee governors stepped down after serving two consecutive terms, and Crump hoped to influence who the 1926 gubernatorial nominee would be. Governor Peay, however, had other ideas. He announced to a startled electorate his decision to run for an unprecedented third term. Regular Democrats rallied around the governor as the 1926 campaign season began, but some were outraged. Perhaps the most notable Tennessean to oppose the third term was grocery store magnate Clarence Saunders, who had played such an important role in Peay's initial gubernatorial bid. Nashville mayor Hilary Howse supported state treasurer Hill McAlister and urged Crump to do the same. "You and I alone can give Hill McAlister twenty to twenty-five thousand majority in Davidson and Shelby Counties . . . ," the Nashville executive reported to Crump.[22] Heeding his advice, Crump supported McAlister in the August Democratic primary.

In order to defeat Peay in Shelby County, machine stalwarts worked to increase voter registration. During a three-day supplemental registration period in July, twenty-five thousand names were added to the voter rolls,[23] which increased the total number of registered voters to fifty thousand.[24] This was accomplished by a highly organized transportation system that carried eligible voters to registration facilities.[25] The county organization was augmented by Clarence Saunders, who endorsed McAlister and excoriated Peay in several full-page newspaper advertisements.[26] Crump and his lieutenants were able to concentrate on the gubernatorial primary because they faced no opposition in the county races, save a nominal opponent to Sheriff Will Knight.[27]

Despite aggressive campaigning and the strong support of Mayor Paine, Peay was unable to carry Shelby County on election day. McAlister polled fifteen thousand votes to the governor's three thousand, giving the machine candidate a twelve-thousand-vote majority. The Crump organization easily reelected Sheriff Knight, which proved again their electoral supremacy in Shelby County. However, the votes tallied for McAlister did not affect the outcome of the statewide contest. Governor Peay was chosen the Democratic nominee and was reelected for a third term in the fall.[28] Perhaps most significantly, the election renewed the hostility that had previously existed between the city and the county. As 1927 began, machine leaders hoped to oppose Mayor Paine in the next municipal election. Without an overriding issue to challenge the city administration, however, their chances seemed rather slim.

The situation changed in the spring of 1927 when federal prohibition agents in Memphis raided a grocery store at the intersection of Fourth and Butler owned by bootlegger John Bellomini. As federal officials rifled thorough the store, they seized an account book that listed names and dollar amounts. When prohibition agents examined the book, they discovered some familiar names. Under the heading "Lege" (Latin for "law") fifty-one police officers, four sheriff's deputies, and several county constables were listed beside dollar amounts that ranged from five to twenty dollars. There were also entries labeled "Sheriffs' Department" and "Government."[29] Police inspector Mike Kehoe learned of the evidence and reported the information to fire and police commissioner Thomas H. Allen. Meeting with U. S. district attorney Lindsay B. Phillips, Allen requested a federal investigation, but Phillips inexplicably convinced him they should wait.[30] For unclear reasons they also decided not to inform Mayor Paine of the situation. They could not, however, keep the lid on forever.

In late June rumors began to circulate that the police department was enmeshed in some kind of scandal. A newspaper reporter alerted Mayor Paine, who then requested that federal judge Harry B. Anderson call a special session of the federal grand jury to investigate the matter. "The federal government has the best facilities for making such an investigation," the mayor announced.[31] Paine was acutely aware that any local investigation would be conducted by Crump stalwart W. Tyler McLain. As already mentioned, the organization was hamstrung because there was no major issue with which to attack the city administration. Now they had one.

The first volley was launched by Attorney General McLain, who described Paine's administration as an "inefficient and tottering city government." McLain then urged the mayor to "lay aside any thought of politics this fall, and begin an investigation. . . ."[32] If Paine and Commissioner Allen did not conduct their own investigation, the attorney general threatened to remove them from office.[33] Mayor Paine responded that he trusted the federal government a great deal more than the attorney general's office.[34] Concerned that Judge Anderson had not answered his call for an investigation, Paine secretly traveled to the nation's capital, where he consulted with justice department officials.[35]

The mayor received Judge Anderson's decision soon after his return from Washington. "Unless a conspiracy to violate the National Prohibition Act could be predicted on these alleged payments, it is difficult for me to see what federal crime was committed. . . . [T]his is a case properly within the jurisdiction of the Shelby County Criminal Court and the Shelby County Grand Jury," Anderson wrote.[36]

Federal officials were not the only ones to break with Paine. The local Methodist Pastors' Association adopted a resolution calling for an investigation of the police department,[37] while the City Club began an inquiry of their own.[38] Although the City Club had once allied with the county leader, by 1927 they were staunch supporters of the Paine administration. Club members earned the wrath of the county machine when they supported Governor Peay's attempt to expand the size of the state election commission in 1923. In a letter to Senator McKellar, Crump described club leaders as political failures who "have incurable cases of soreheadedness."[39]

City Club members may or may not have been political soreheads, but some were irked over the club's involvement in the scandal. Insurance broker A. E. Pipkin informed committee members that the evidence in the payoff book was undoubtedly a forgery designed to embarrass the Paine administration. Despite Pipkin's opposition, the investigating committee of the City Club met with Paine and Allen, who assured them of their cooperation. The mayor and commissioner agreed to provide a transcript of the alleged payoff book, but later reneged.[40] Several people came forward with allegations against the police department but, without direct evidence, the investigation ground to a halt.

The final report of the committee was read to the membership and adopted on July 30. The committee concluded that the Bellomini ledger was genuine, that Commissioner Allen should not have refused the club's request to see the book, and that the police department was riddled with corruption and a thorough investigation should be conducted by both county and federal grand juries.[41] As the report was being read by attorney Floyd Creasy, Pipkin roared in anger, "[Y]ou're a liar by the clock!" The insurance broker then grabbed a catsup bottle and was about to hurl it at Creasy when he was restrained by other members.[42]

The City Club report did little to resolve the problem of corruption in the Memphis Police Department, but it did signal a shift in local politics. For the first time, a large segment of the progressive reform bloc slipped from Rowlett Paine's orbit. This development was not lost on Crump and his lieutenants, who quietly laid plans to challenge the mayor in the fall municipal election.[43] Stung by the criticism and lack of support, Paine directed Memphis businessman and former Justice Department operative Jack Ettlinger to inquire into the bribery scandal.[44] Local prohibition agents were also active. In mid-August deputy prohibition administrator Alvin J. Howe, with Ettlinger's assistance, arrested Bellomini, his bookkeeper,

Joe Rinaldi, and four African Americans for violating the national prohibition act. Arrest warrants were also issued for Bellomini associates Narico Vannucci and Dino Chiochetti, but they fled Memphis before being served.[45]

This was not the first time John Bellomini had seen the inside of a cell. In 1922 he was found guilty of selling narcotics and two years later was convicted of violating the prohibition act. Despite the seriousness of his crimes, his only punishment for both convictions was a nominal fine.[46] The gangster's latest arrest answered the demands of middle-class whites while forcefully countering the allegations of the county machine. In a statement to the press Allen remarked: "We have gone far enough to be certain that the book is a genuine record of some bribery transactions; that some of the police officers named in it are guilty of taking graft. . . ."[47] Undeterred, the county machine announced their slate of candidates for the municipal election a mere four days after Bellomini's incarceration.

Crump's slate was headed by former state legislator and attorney Watkins Overton as the candidate for mayor. Joining Overton on the ticket was city judge Clifford Davis, former school board member Anthony P. Walsh, labor leader O. I. Kruger, and YMCA secretary Sam Jackson.[48] The ticket was in keeping with Crump's philosophy of inclusion, with workers, middle-class reformers, and businessmen represented.[49] Styling themselves the "People's Ticket," the Crump/Overton forces mailed circulars to voters criticizing the city's high tax rate.[50] On August 31, Paine announced his candidacy for a third term and wasted no time in attacking the county organization. "I am opposed to government by proxy. I hold that the seat of the city government ought to be in city hall, not in the private office of a political boss."[51]

The city and county organizations took different approaches to building support for their slate of candidates. Paine forces held a large mass meeting to plan strategy and sent letters to voters urging them to pay their poll tax,[52] while the county machine organized Overton clubs at the ward and neighborhood levels.[53] Voter registration increased during the regular and supplemental registration periods in August and October, with the highest numbers coming from the African American wards and the white middle-class neighborhoods in the eastern sections of the city.[54]

Orchestrating the high black turnout was the West Tennessee Civic and Political League.[55] Formed by black Republican leaders Robert Church, Jr., George W. Lee, and M. S. Stuart, the league marshaled the black vote to influence the outcome of the election. Rallies were held in black neighborhoods, where leaders urged citizens to register. Roscoe Conkling Simmons returned to Memphis, where he exhorted African Americans to vote, which would create "an atmosphere in this city that will make decency and self-respect possible for you."[56] At the end of the registration period, eleven thousand African Americans had registered to vote.[57] The league began their work before either faction proclaimed their ticket, and they remained publicly silent when the rival slates were announced.

Privately, however, the league hoped to exchange their votes for the hiring of African American police officers to patrol black neighborhoods, access to Overton Park Zoo, and higher salaries for black teachers.[58] Crump was aware that black leaders were angry at Paine for building a city crematory near Booker T. Washington High School over their vociferous protest. Consequently he sent Frank Rice to meet with Church, where he promised consideration of their platform.[59] An agreement was apparently reached, for Crump predicted in a newspaper interview that "99.1 per cent" of the African American vote would be cast for Overton.[60] Crump was also emboldened by the endorsement of the City Federation of Colored Women's Clubs president, Mrs. T. S. Brown.[61] Leaving no opportunity unexploited, the county leader urged Mrs. Brown to "impress upon the members of your organizations the necessity of paying their poll taxes...."[62]

Mayor Paine feigned alarm when he read the league platform and Crump's statement. Arguing that the alliance between Church and Crump was "the greatest menace to white supremacy in this city since reconstruction days [,]" Paine went on to state: "There are many intelligent, law-abiding negroes in Memphis, and there is nothing to fear from votes of this class. . . . It is a vastly different situation, however, when a negro political club has been organized with the thought that it can dominate the politics of the City of Memphis and no white man whose political morality is above the level of the carpetbagger, will give aid and comfort to a political organization of negroes that has as its principal object the control of city elections with the solid negro vote."[63]

Alarm spread within the Crump organization that white voters would close ranks with Paine to bolster white supremacy and doom Overton's candidacy. The county organization attempted to blunt the issue by reminding voters that Paine had courted the black vote in 1923. The Overton forces then backed away from any commitments they had previously made: "We do not favor anything which may create race friction, therefore are opposed to negro police, negro firemen, and general admission to the white parks."[64] They pledged, however, to increase the number of parks, swimming pools, and health facilities for African Americans.[65] In other words, Overton promised separate but equal access to city services. Overton's pronouncement dampened the hopes of the black leadership but they were left with little choice. Meeting at Beale Avenue Baptist Church, the West Tennessee Civic and Political League formally endorsed the machine ticket.[66]

Meanwhile, the bribery investigation ground on. A former Bellomini employee, Gus Bocchini, was arrested in Chicago and agreed to testify against his former boss in exchange for immunity.[67] Faced with the probability that no federal indictments would be handed down, Commissioner Allen charged forty-one police officers

with inefficiency, incompetency, and conduct unbecoming an officer and suspended them from duty. Because the officers were civil servants, a review by police trial boards were required for the suspensions to be permanent. In explaining his decision, Allen stated: "The investigation has now reached a point where I am convinced that the book is a genuine record of the monetary transactions of the Bellomini crowd. . . . My duty is, therefore, plain. It is unfortunate that it must be performed in the midst of a political campaign."[68] Unfortunate or not, the suspensions immediately became an election issue.

Soon after the police commissioner's announcement, a member of the police department charged that officers were pressured to actively support the Paine ticket or risk losing their jobs.[69] In response to this charge, Detective E. M. Crumby resigned.[70] Further proof of coercion came two days later when Allen suspended Captain Will Lee for "inefficiency" because he "failed to suppress the illegal sale of intoxicating liquors by John Bellomini."[71] Lee countered that Allen had asked for his resignation but promised to "delay action in my case until I went to Mayor Paine and told the mayor how I stood politically." In his statement to the newspapers, Lee vowed he would never "tell either Mayor Paine or Commissioner [Allen] how I stand politically."[72] Considerable damage was done to the Paine campaign as the suspended police officers (and their coworkers) quietly joined the Crump/Overton faction. At a twenty-ninth ward rally for the Overton ticket, Captain Lee was introduced to an enthusiastic crowd.[73]

The city assembled the police trial board, made up of assistant chief John W. Plaxo, deputy inspector Edward A. Parker, and Captain W. J. Herrington, who began hearing evidence about the officers' inefficiency in early October. Prosecuting the case was assistant city attorney John L. Exby, who began the proceedings by stating he was not going to prove the officers received graft. He then called Bellomini employees Gus Bocchini and John Dorsey, who testified that they witnessed frequent visits to the store by several of the accused.[74] Bookkeeper Joe Rinaldi confirmed he did write some of the entries in the payoff book, but did not implicate any of the officers.[75] Introducing the ledger into evidence, Exby argued that it proved police officers were aware of Bellomini's criminal enterprise but did nothing to suppress it.[76]

Defense attorney Charles M. Bryan called Sergeant W. E. Adams to the stand, where he testified that Bellomini's store was closely monitored and had been raided by the Memphis police.[77] Bryan argued that the ledger included fake entries used by fugitives Narico Vanucci and Dino Chiochetti to swindle money from Bellomini.[78] Chastising the prosecution, Bryan declared: "There is no use mincing questions or disguising the issue. You are really charging these men with bribery. Yet you have closed your case without showing that one member of the police force received so much as a dime."[79] The defense rested after pointing out that seven officers mentioned in the book remained on the force, implying they were protected for political reasons.[80] It did not take long for the trial board to see the contradiction in the prosecution's case and rule that the accused were not guilty.[81] Commissioner Allen was slow to return the men to duty, however, with the bulk of them not being reinstated until after the election.[82] Several days later John Bellomini pled guilty to violating the prohibition act and was sentenced to six months in jail, bringing to an end the scandal that bore his name. Or did it? For many voters, the scandal was far from over.

The middle class remained disgusted by Paine's handling of the whole affair, while the Crump/Overton forces exploited this anger. In a campaign advertisement, Overton rhetorically asked the mayor: "Why don't you give Captain Lee and the 38 policemen a square deal? They haven't had it from you, and are not getting it, or they would be back at work."[83] Paine continued to argue that the Crump ticket undermined white rule,[84] but few were listening.

As we already know, Crump had alienated middle-class reformers in the past, but by the fall of 1927 much had changed. Alliances shifted so strongly that the middle class even joined ranks with anti-Crump Democrats to endorse the Overton slate.[85] The names of thousands of pledged voters were collected and their support was advertised by the county organization.[86] The most prominent antimachine leader to support Overton was former mayor Harry Litty, who had challenged Crump in the 1916 county trustee's race. Middle-class disaffection spread to the city bureaucracy as several officials, most notably city engineer William B. Fowler, fled to the opposition and supported the organization ticket.[87] Shocked by these events, Paine lashed out at Crump: "Everybody in Memphis who knows anything about politics knows that Watkins Overton is simply a proxy for E. H. Crump; that he dare not do or say a thing until E. H. Crump approves it."[88] But it was not enough. The twin specters of bossism and black supremacy failed to sway voters, as evidenced by the results on election day.

The county machine slate overwhelmed the incumbent administration with Watkins Overton receiving 19,548 votes to Paine's 6,948.[89] The organizational skill of Crump and his lieutenants was clearly evident when a fleet of automobiles transported voters to the polls.[90] To the surprise of political insiders, the majority of votes for the Crump ticket were cast not only in African American neighborhoods and white working-class sections of north and south Memphis, but also from the middle-class enclaves on the eastern edge of the city.[91] Asked to comment, Crump merely replied, "[T]he people have made their statement."[92] Wearing a new suit and hat, Crump linked arms with Overton and Clifford Davis and led a march of supporters through downtown streets as a band played "There'll Be a Hot Time in the Old Town Tonight." Included in the parade ranks were many of the exonerated police officers.[93] This impromptu demonstration signaled a new era in Memphis politics. After twelve years of struggle, Crump had unified Memphis and Shelby County into a coherent political force.

"A Good Tammany Hall Tennessean"

When Watkins Overton was inaugurated mayor in January 1928, the city government of Memphis was absorbed by the Shelby County Democratic organization. The political fracture that stretched back to 1915 was healed through the merger of county machine and city government, in effect creating a consolidated city/county government. Crump was head of this combined government, with the mayor acting as his chief advisor. Other high-ranking members of the organization were county commission chairman E. W. Hale, county attorney general W. Tyler McLain, and Frank Rice. Crump relied heavily on their counsel, referring to these men as the "generalissimos."

Crump and his chief generalissimo met three hours after the inauguration to discuss future plans. Several promises for civic improvement had been outlined in a twenty-six-point platform, and they began implementing them immediately. For example, Overton had pledged to establish "a municipal airport, centrally located and easily accessible."[1] An airport commission was formed to advise city leaders on the "feasibility and practicability of a public airport for Memphis."[2] A site was secured,[3] and the Memphis Municipal Airport was constructed the following year.[4] Naturally there was little opposition to a construction project that brought increased commerce to the city, but the new administration faced a more complicated situation when it tried to reduce lawless behavior.

Crime played a major role in Memphis's culture and politics, as evidenced by the Bellomini scandal that helped bring Overton to power. During the 1920s Dr. Frederick L. Hoffman, the statistician for the Prudential Insurance Company, labeled Memphis the murder capital of the United States,[5] and Crump was determined to repair this image. No doubt he also wanted to dispel the perception that he was soft on crime. This was difficult given his lack of enthusiasm for enforcing prohibition and the support his organization received from the underworld. Many saloon owners proudly referred to themselves as "paid up" members of the machine, which rankled reform elements within the organization. Overton and police commissioner Clifford Davis struck hard at organized crime. Liquor and gambling establishments were successfully raided by the police, who confiscated 1,200 gallons of illegal whiskey.[6]

"Paid up" saloonkeepers angrily demanded Davis's removal, but Crump and Overton supported the commissioner. "We would like to help our friends, but we can't let them violate the law," Overton stated to the press.[7] In a further attempt to curb lawlessness, Davis reorganized the police department by rotating every patrolman to a new ward.[8] Ten days later, in an attempt to avoid the mistakes of the Paine administration, detective sergeants Mario Chiozza and Morris Solomon were demoted after Davis saw them at a "questionable place."[9] The white middle class, whose votes were far more important than the underworld's money, were greatly relieved when the new administration struck at the criminal element. As we shall see, this was but the opening round of a struggle that would dominate Memphis politics for years to come.

Controlling the raucous tendencies of some Memphians involved not only law enforcement, but also government-mandated censorship. As already discussed in chapter one, Crump established a board of censors that once prevented a racially sensitive play from being performed in Memphis. His fear that popular culture might spark racial violence remained and colored his actions as party leader. Overton appointed Columbian Mutual Life Insurance Company president Lloyd T. Binford chairman of the board of censors. The new chair was soon embroiled in controversy. In March 1928 the Lyric Theater began showing Cecil B. DeMille's epic film of the life of Christ, *King of Kings*. Local Jewish leaders, mirroring their counterparts throughout the nation, objected to the film on the grounds that it was anti-Semitic.

Concerned the film might spark an incident, Binford declared several sequences in the film were "a perversion of the true life of Christ and one of the worst travesties on the Bible I have ever seen" and ordered them deleted.[10] The manager of the Lyric, Vincent Carline, refused to comply and was arrested.[11] A lawsuit was filed in circuit court, which ruled in favor of the theater management. Judge A. B. Pittman stated that "there is nothing in this screen version of the life of Christ that is likely to stir up religious hatred or prove inimical to public welfare."[12] City attorney Walter Chandler appealed the decision and was affirmed in his argument that the censor board was duly constituted and did not exceed its authority. Unwilling to accept the decision of the court of appeals, the Lyric management took their suit to the Tennessee Supreme Court, which refused to hear the case.[13]

The action taken against *King of Kings* continued the precedent established when *The Leopard's Spots* was banned in 1914. Jews, like African Americans, were a significant part of the electorate. Several members of the Jewish community were highly visible political advisors, most notably assistant attorney general Will Gerber.[14] Racial violence against Jews was not unknown in the South. Crump was aware of the 1915 lynching of Leo Frank in Atlanta after his conviction for the murder of Mary Phagan. Shortly before Frank's lynching, Crump appealed to Georgia governor J. H. Slaton for clemency[15] on the advice of Jewish merchant A. L. Lowenstein.[16] Frank's lynching almost certainly influenced Binford in his suppression of *King of Kings*.

This process continued for the rest of Crump's political career. In 1936, for example, the Memphis Board of Censors prevented the screening of the prizefight between African American boxer Joe Louis and Max Schmelling.[17] Fearing that the image of a Caucasian fighter pummeling an African American would spark white violence, the board passed a resolution banning all boxing films "regardless of whether or not the participants in the fight were white or colored."[18] Binford was widely criticized for sanitizing Memphis's movie screens. *Collier's* magazine stated: "Censorship, Memphis-Binford style, concededly provides an extreme case of capricious and mischievous interference with the freedom of adults"[19] and film producer Samuel Goldwyn rhetorically asked during an interview with famed Hollywood gossip columnist Hedda Hopper: "How can people of Memphis tolerate such a man as Binford?"[20] He was tolerated because Crump saw the value in censoring films to prevent disorder.[21]

With the city/county organization solidly under his command, Crump hoped to further expand his influence in Nashville. In 1927, Governor Peay unexpectedly died in the midst of his unprecedented third term. He was succeeded by senate speaker Henry Horton, who did not get along with Crump any better than his predecessor. Hoping to unseat Horton, Shelby County Democrats supported state treasurer Hill McAlister in the August 1928 Democratic primary. The organization formed a campaign committee of 1700 men and women, and they secured the endorsement of nearly every major voting bloc in Shelby County.[22] Desperate to control the vote, the Crump faithful resorted to extraordinary means to achieve electoral success. In order to pad the total vote count, loyal poll workers marked ballots and placed them in ballot boxes throughout the county.[23] As they attempted to enter polling places, newspaper reporters were assaulted, and others were detained by the police.[24] Crump loyalist Will Gerber joined in the melee when he slapped and cursed an *Evening Appeal* reporter.[25] Warrants were sworn out against several police officers and Gerber, but the grand jury failed to indict any of them.[26]

Given the antidemocratic nature of the violence and intimidation used by the machine, the question then becomes whether these were the actions of a handful of rogue agents or of people who were acting on orders from above. The involvement of Gerber, who was then a rising star within the machine, suggests that Crump condoned their actions and probably gave permission to carry them out. The fact that the Shelby County grand jury refused to indict Gerber and the others is further evidence that the leaders of the organization approved of the violence practiced in 1928.

The organization's tactics worked within Shelby County. McAlister polled 24,069 votes, while Horton received only 3,693. However, the city/county machine was still in a formative stage and failed to poll enough votes to influence the statewide outcome of the primary. Consequently, Horton defeated McAlister by 4,264 votes.[27] Despite this, the Shelby County electoral apparatus was firmly in Crump's hands. The organization's slate once again won all county offices in the county general election held at the same time as the primary.

Having proved the far-reaching powers of the unified machine, the leadership again increased public services. A harbor commission was created to expand Memphis's role in waterborne commerce,[28] and Jefferson Davis Park was constructed on the riverfront.[29] Expanding local government as a means of enhancing the prestige of the machine became difficult to do as the country experienced the effects of the Great Depression. At first the city weathered the economic collapse fairly well. In the spring of 1930 unemployment was only 2 percent for whites and 3 percent for blacks. This did not last long, though. By the end of the year thousands had lost their jobs.[30]

Not wanting to appear ineffective, the organization created the Mayor's Commission on Employment and Relief in December 1930. During its two years of operation it helped hundreds find temporary work and distributed food and clothing to the most destitute.[31] The commission did little to halt the spread of economic despair, but it did convince some that the machine was doing all it could to help the victims of financial disaster. The reason the city could not do more was due primarily to an inability to collect taxes owed. Despite a relatively low tax rate, many of the larger property owners were unable to pay and formed the Property Owners Association to block the city's attempt at collecting back taxes. Through a combination of refusal and litigation, the property owners prevented the city from collecting taxes due. By 1933, $4.6 million was owed the city.[32] The Property Owners Association was not merely a fiscal danger to Memphis; it was also a political threat to the Crump organization.

Nevertheless, with the city/county organization running smoothly under the able leadership of Mayor Overton and the other generalissimos, Crump had little to do. Boredom, as well as a desire to expand his political influence beyond Tennessee, almost certainly led him to run for the U.S. Congress in 1930. The seat for the tenth congressional district was then occupied by Hubert Fisher, who had served in that capacity for sixteen years. Crump consulted with the generalissimos and sent Hale to Washington to talk to Fisher and McKellar.[33] In a telegram Senator McKellar expressed the view that "it would give me the greatest pleasure and satisfaction in the world to have you as a colleague and associate here."[34] Fisher bowed to Crump's wishes and agreed to step down.

In announcing his candidacy, Crump promised to help farmers, workers, and veterans grappling with the effects of the Great Depression. Crump also pledged to secure government assistance to combat malaria in the Mississippi Valley, and increase health care services for African Americans.[35] Nearly every major voting bloc was represented in the announcement of his platform, and all rushed to support his election. It was felt by many that Crump would be able to increase federal assistance to depression-ravaged Shelby County.[36] The date set for candidates to file for the November election passed without anyone opposing Crump. This meant his election was assured, but much more was at stake than one congressional seat. In early 1930 Crump struck a deal with former U.S. senator and newspaper publisher Luke Lea, who had emerged in the 1920s as the undisputed leader of Tennessee politics. In exchange for supporting Governor Horton's reelection bid, Crump received a percentage of state patronage and increased road building in Shelby County.[37]

Organization workers fanned out across the city and county, urging eligible voters to register and pay their poll tax. When the registration period closed, 62,220 citizens had registered to vote, the largest in Shelby County history up to that time.[38] Whether or not Memphians felt any loyalty to Crump, the large number of registered voters suggests not only the organizational skills of the machine, but also the high level of citizen participation in civic affairs during the Great Depression. One of the most important outlets for citizen involvement was through the twenty-four civic clubs active in Memphis neighborhoods. By the mid-1920s, most of the larger white communities had established a civic club to promote their neighborhood interests.[39] Realizing the benefits of coordination, the individual clubs established the Memphis Council of Civic Clubs, which brought all the neighborhoods together under the leadership of a nine-member board.[40]

The council was formed in 1928, the same year the county organization merged with city government, and the two groups worked closely together. The ten thousand members of the civic clubs worked with city government to combat the Great Depression, sponsored fire prevention weeks in conjunction with the fire and police commissioner and funneled requests to the city commission.[41] Although officially nonpolitical, the civic clubs' support of the administration strengthened the machine's position on the neighborhood level. Because of their large numbers—ten thousand members in 1935—[42] the civic clubs acted as a kind of check and balance on the more unsavory aspects of the machine. Realizing this, Crump and the generalissimos paid a great deal of attention to the white civic clubs.[43]

African Americans were also very active in civic affairs. Black civic clubs were organized and acted in the same way as their white counterparts. Groups like the Orange Mound Civic Club and the East End Progressive Club strived for neighborhood improvements for middle-class black homeowners and conducted voter registration drives.[44] In 1930 African Americans petitioned for more recreational facilities, which led to the construction of Beale Avenue Park the following year.[45] Along similar lines, in the summer of 1933 Robert Church, Jr., was arrested for reckless driving. Boasting to the police that he was "as good" as they were, Church risked incurring the violent wrath of white officers. Instead of his being beaten, the charges were dropped without Church ever entering a courtroom.[46] In a similar vein, Church's protégé George W. Lee convinced the city commission to rename Beale Avenue Park to honor W. C. Handy, despite initial objections from Crump.[47]

Opening the formal campaign for the August primary, Crump and the Shelby County organization hosted a free party for all white Memphians at the Fairgrounds Amusement Park on July 25. Forty thousand citizens jammed the fairgrounds to dance, race, and ride amusement park rides. Entertainment during the day included watching members of the city commission compete in a mule race and riding the merry-go-round with Crump, generalissimos McLain and Hale, and Sheriff Will Bacon. Crump walked among the crowds, and it was reported he called by name three thousand of the forty thousand who attended.[48] That was almost certainly an exaggeration, but it does speak to the charm Crump used so effectively to win over the voters of Shelby County. Undoubtedly, the machine hoped that when it came time to vote on primary day the attendees would remember how well they were treated at the fairgrounds.

The party faithful did not have long to wait. The strength of the organization was confirmed when the Democratic voters of Shelby County gave Governor Horton twenty-five thousand votes on August 8, securing his nomination and subsequent reelection. There was no Democratic opposition to Crump so he became the automatic nominee for Congress.[49] Despite the comfortable majority earned in the primary, and the relative weakness of Shelby County Republicans, the organization took nothing for granted. Ward meetings were held across the county to stir the party faithful. Several large rallies were held, including one in North Memphis that attracted five thousand enthusiastic Crump supporters.[50]

The machine even received support from an unlikely source. Two weeks after the August primary Overton traveled to Washington for a meeting with President Herbert Hoover. The conference was in reply to the mayor's suggestion that flood control projects on the Mississippi River be increased to help alleviate the appalling lack of employment in Memphis. Hoover reacted favorably to the mayor's suggestion, doubling the appropriation to seventy million dollars.[51] Having directed federal relief efforts in Memphis during the 1927 Mississippi River flood, Hoover, as president, strongly supported flood control measures.[52] Crump and his organization proved by these negotiations that they were powerful enough to squeeze federal funds from a tightfisted, recalcitrant president like Herbert Hoover.

In the midst of the general election, a potential stumbling block to Crump's aspirations appeared when Republican U. S. senator Gerald Nye, chairman of the campaign funds committee, arrived in

Memphis to investigate corruption charges in the August primary. Allegations had been made that wholesale fraud had occurred in several Tennessee counties, including Shelby. Nye and his committee, which included Democratic senator Robert Wagner of New York, specifically investigated the senatorial nomination of Cordell Hull. Despite the allegations, Nye found no evidence the election was tainted. At the end of the hearing Nye replied that there was "no substantial ground for the serious charges brought in Tennessee."[53] The election of Hull was of little importance to the Shelby County organization. The real battle was for the governorship, which the U. S. Senate had no jurisdiction to investigate. As Crump wrote to McKellar, "[W]e took no part in the senatorial contest."[54]

Wanting to deliver a large majority for Crump and Governor Horton, ward and precinct workers redoubled their efforts. In order to demonstrate the invincibility of the machine, Crump needed to amass a large majority not only for Horton, but for himself as well. He did not need a large majority to win the congressional seat, but it was necessary to demonstrate he could deliver a block of votes for any candidate of his choosing. Ward meetings were held in every section of the city to plot strategy, while at large public rallies organization leaders exhorted citizens to vote.[55]

When the people went to the polls on November 4, the efficiency of the machine was clearly revealed. Crump received 23,753 votes, giving him a 15 to 1 majority over Republican Herbert Harper and independent Tom Collier of the Property Owners Association. Horton's total was slightly less, 21,747, but he outpolled Republican Arthur Bruce by 18,000 votes.[56] The election of Horton signaled a shift in the political balance of power in Tennessee. It was true that Governor Horton owed his primary allegiance to the rural/prohibitionist bloc dominated by Luke Lea, but the election of 1930 revealed the considerable impact the Shelby County vote had on the political process of the state. For the next eighteen years it would be impossible for a gubernatorial candidate to win without the support of the Crump machine.

Economic events related to the Great Depression shattered the alliance that had existed between Crump, Lea, and Horton. Three days after the election, state government lost $6,659,000 in deposits when several banks owned by Rogers Caldwell collapsed. A close ally and partner of Lea, Caldwell owned a financial empire that was thrown into receivership one week after the bank failures. State finances were thus in disarray just as the effects of depression were beginning to be felt in Tennessee. Horton was quickly blamed. A committee of anti-Horton Democrats formed to put pressure on the incoming legislature to investigate the disaster, while mass meetings were held across the state to denounce Horton and Lea.[57]

One city that did not hold a public demonstration was Memphis. Crump traveled to Nashville at the start of the 1931 legislative session where he met with anti-Horton Democrats who wanted his support for their proposed investigation. But Crump had his own agenda. The Memphis leader wanted Shelby County senator Scott Fitzhugh named speaker of the senate; to the surprise of no one, the two factions quickly reached an accommodation. After Fitzhugh's election, Crump and the Shelby delegation were instrumental in the creation of an investigating committee.[58] "We were very successful in Nashville, winning everything, and the investigation is all set for an extraordinary, determined and thorough search and research of everything and everybody connected with state affairs," Crump wrote.[59] To political observers throughout the state, these actions meant Crump was the new boss of Tennessee.[60]

The investigation of state finances uncovered mismanagement of funds, but a drive to impeach the governor was stopped cold by Horton and his allies. Although recognized as the most powerful leader in the state, Crump was unable to remove Horton from office. The most important reason the legislature rejected impeachment was the loathing felt for the congressman-elect from Memphis. Many rural Democrats from around the state simply refused to support any measure associated with Crump, despite the shoddy conditions of the state treasury.[61]

Traveling to Washington in May, the freshman congressman conferred with post office officials regarding the extension of air mail service to Memphis, and discussed the possibility of being appointed to the House Military Affairs Committee with Mississippi representative Percy Quin.[62] Crump issued a statement supporting President Hoover's plan to combat the Depression by postponing the collection of debts incurred by Europe during the Great War.[63] In a letter to Memphis attorney and American Legion leader Roane Waring, the congressman declared: "When the whole world is in trouble it is not time for narrow partisan snarls."[64] Despite these activities, there was little for Crump to do until Congress convened in December 1931.

Although the congressman had emerged as the most powerful political leader in Memphis and Shelby County, this did not mean every citizen paid allegiance to him. In 1931 Watkins Overton ran for reelection, and, despite his successes, it was not certain Overton would win. A potential setback occurred when an anti-Crump Democrat, Rembert Moon, was appointed to the county election commission. The commission, chaired by organization Democrat Roane Waring, also included Republican J. R. Townsend. In local elections Republicans tended to support Crump Democrats, and this was also true on the election board. Despite protests from Moon, who exclaimed in frustration that the other members were "objecting to all my appointees," Crump forces secured 60 percent of the available registrar posts.[65] This meant over half of those registering eligible voters owed their allegiance to the organization. When the registration period ended, 58,706 citizens were able to cast ballots. Of that number, 24,086 were African American.[66]

Meanwhile, a small group of angry property owners and disaffected Democrats banded together as the Voters League to oppose the administration.[67] Unable at first to find a suitable candidate to oppose Overton, the league became little more than an outlet for a few to vent their frustration over high taxes and black voting. The league eventually found a mayoral candidate in former city clerk C. C. Pashby, who, with a handful of league stalwarts, tried in vain to establish an anti-Crump coalition.[68] Ignored by the citizens they desperately wanted to serve, the Voters League watched helplessly as the administration picked up the endorsement of every major voting bloc in the city. Ward workers prepared for election day, but there were no public rallies or speeches by the candidates.[69] They were not needed. Without a viable opposition, the administration won handily. Overton received 23,000 votes, the largest total ever recorded in a municipal election up to that time.[70]

With his Memphis base secure, Congressman Crump traveled to Washington at the end of November to assume his new duties. He was named a member of the House Military Affairs Committee, where he played an important role in determining the fate of the stalled Muscle Shoals public power project, the forerunner of the Tennessee Valley Authority. During his first year in Congress Crump introduced a bill to increase funds to public health agencies combating malaria in the Mississippi Valley,[71] supported the immediate payment of bonuses owed World War I veterans,[72] and lined up key votes which secured Tennessean Joseph Byrns's election as House majority leader.[73] Crump also joined seventy-one other Democrats in voting for House Speaker John Nance Garner's $2.5 billion emergency relief and public works bill.[74] While in Congress Crump kept in close touch with the generalissimos and relied heavily on their advice. "Regarding the bonus, you recall I talked with you boys about it and you all thought it the part of wisdom for me to vote for it, which I am inclined to do," the freshman congressman wrote the mayor in 1932.[75] City agencies became adjuncts to Crump's congressional office; the health department, for example, sent a weekly list of all newborn babies to the congressman's office, which then mailed a government publication on child care to their parents.[76]

Service in Washington apparently convinced Crump he was on the cusp of wielding national power. The crucial election year of 1932 potentially offered the freshman congressman just such an opportunity. In the fall of 1931 Crump publicly stated that Democratic New York governor Franklin D. Roosevelt was the best candidate to challenge Herbert Hoover for the presidency in 1932: "Any man who has the nerve to conquer the disease with which Governor Roosevelt was afflicted must certainly have the stamina to wrest this country from the Republican depression."[77] Following Crump's lead, the Shelby organization formed a Roosevelt for President Club. Hoping to play a major role in Roosevelt's campaign, Crump wrote to the executive's personal secretary in October promising to "perfect an organization for Governor Roosevelt for president" and asking for a list of the governor's accomplishments.[78] However, the Roosevelt campaign was unaware of Crump and his Memphis organization. Fearing Crump might damage Roosevelt's candidacy, the governor's personal secretary, Louis Howe, asked Senator Cordell Hull for advice on dealing with the congressman.[79] Six weeks later Howe replied by sending Crump a recently published biography of Roosevelt.[80] Frustrated with his inability to get to Roosevelt, Crump waited another six weeks and then replied: "Was there any good reason why it should have taken you more than one month to reply to what I thought a very courteous letter based on my sincere interest in Governor Roosevelt?"[81]

Realizing their mistake, Roosevelt sent word to Crump through former Tennessee house speaker Clyde Shropshire that he was aware of the Memphis congressman's political activities and was very grateful.[82] In March Roosevelt asked Crump to come to New York to discuss the upcoming presidential campaign.[83] Still smarting over his earlier experience, the Memphis Democrat was in an uncooperative mood: "I am going along for you, inasmuch as I started out that way. However, I must be perfectly frank in saying that, in the light of the gratuitous treatment I received, I just cannot accept your invitation."[84] The congressman confided in Overton that "I can see defects in Governor Roosevelt's make up...."[85] Desperate to assuage Crump's bitter feelings, Roosevelt wrote to him again in May: "I am indeed grateful to you for all that you have done. I should much like to have a good talk with you before you go to Chicago. Can you not run up to see me either in Albany or in Hyde Park...? There are many things I should like to talk over with you."[86] This time Crump relented, traveling to Hyde Park on the eve of the convention.[87]

Serving as a delegate to the Democratic National Convention in 1932, Crump was instrumental in securing Tennessee's twenty-four votes for Roosevelt on the first ballot.[88] However, in September tension again flared between the two when Roosevelt was unable to honor Crump's request to speak in Memphis.[89] Despite this rift, Roosevelt received 38,053 votes in Shelby County to Hoover's 5,990.[90] Roosevelt's overwhelming victory in Shelby County helped him win Tennessee by 221,832 votes.[91] After Roosevelt's inauguration, Crump and other members of the Tennessee congressional delegation met with the newly elected president in the White House. During the meeting Roosevelt turned to Crump and said he was reminded of the campaign when the Memphis congressman was "terribly provoked" because he did not visit Tennessee. Crump looked at the president and asked, "Have you any censure for what I did for you in Chicago?" Roosevelt smiled and said "no." Perhaps believing Crump was offended, the president praised him as "a good Tammany Hall Tennessean" who "usually got results."[92] The 1932 campaign was an unsettling experience for the Memphis leader. Despite his support for Roosevelt, he was deeply disappointed, and it showed in his fractured relationship with the new president.

Around the same time Crump became disenchanted with Roosevelt, he was also faced with making a decision on whom to support for Tennessee governor. The Shelby leader wanted to stay out of the fray and concentrate on the presidential contest, but events forced him to act.[93] Specifically, opponents of the county machine began to strike out. In April several hundred members of the Property Owners Association marched on city hall to demand that the city lower the tax rate. Presented with a written pledge to cut taxes, Overton and the commission refused to sign.[94] Not long after the Property Owners Association demonstration, Republicans H. H. Fisher, H. W. Pyle, and George F. Styers founded the Loyal Order of Americans to challenge the county organization in the 1932 elections.[95]

In late June and early July, Pyle and others charged they were being denied access to government flour being distributed to the unemployed by the American Red Cross. Pyle dispatched correspondence to New York congressman Fiorello LaGuardia[96] and President Hoover,[97] while eleven of those who allegedly were denied flour lobbied Red Cross headquarters for an investigation.[98] Sensing an opportunity to weaken Democrats in Tennessee, Republican senator William Borah of Idaho released the letters to the press.[99] The Red Cross denied the charges, while unemployed workers like printer W. F. Ware stated to the press that "no faction has ever approached us" when flour was distributed.[100]

Despite these refutations, Crump could not contain his anger at Borah. "You have done me an irreparable injury and at the same time have offered a gratuitous insult to the integrity and honor of the local officials of the American Red Cross and other charitable agencies of the City of Memphis. The time has come for a showdown."[101] Although unwilling to apologize,[102] Borah was disinclined to fight the Memphis congressman: "I had no personal feeling against you and had no desire to injure anyone. . . ."[103] The reality was he didn't have to fight Crump. It was enough to briefly tarnish a southern Democrat in a crucial election year.

Although the flour incident did not weaken Crump's position, it did lead to a curious alliance between the Republican-backed Loyal Order of Americans, anti-Crump Democrats, and the Property Owners Association. When controversial former governor Malcolm Patterson announced his candidacy,[104] the factions eagerly joined his standard. Remnants of the Horton/Lea axis also supported Patterson, saddling the former governor with their image of mismanagement and corruption. Crump was unwilling to support Patterson, and he did not want to see the divisive former executive win the nomination.

Mayor Overton learned that Hill McAlister wanted to run again, but he and the other generalissimos were unenthusiastic.[105] It was hoped that someone else would seek the governorship, but by early summer no one had appeared to challenge either candidate. Crump lamented that "McAlister is a good man. But I've never been able to convince myself that he can put any real life and fire into the campaign. . . ."[106] However, he had little choice. The organization eventually endorsed McAlister in hopes of crushing both Patterson and the antimachine voters in Shelby County.[107]

Determined to prove their political strength to both state and national observers, the organization rushed to increase voter registration. In April deputies and constables were issued poll tax books to collect the two-dollar payment for voting in Tennessee.[108] The use of uniformed law enforcement officials to collect poll taxes must have intimidated some voters, but it was a useful tactic. Over 92,000 Shelby County residents registered,[109] a remarkable figure given that the total population of Shelby County was 306,482.[110] At least 35,000 of those voters were African American, which continued to dismay anti-Crump Democrats across Tennessee. At a raucous state executive committee meeting in July, a resolution condemning black voting was adopted, but preventative measures were not enacted.[111] Concerned that Patterson loyalists would try to document black voting, Commissioner Davis ordered police to "advise citizens not to take pictures" at polling places.[112] On primary day, Crump warned newspaper reporters that if he discovered anyone taking "fake" pictures of African American voters, he would "throw his camera across the street and have him arrested."[113] Police followed up this warning by destroying the cameras of newspapermen and beating anti-Crump voters.[114] These tactics worked. On primary day, Shelby voters ensured the nomination of McAlister by delivering thirty-one thousand votes,[115] which in turn led to his election in the fall.[116]

The elections of Roosevelt and McAlister in the fall of 1932 secured for the Shelby County organization an enormous amount of prestige. In particular, their success provided Memphis with more resources to combat the Great Depression. By the end of the decade, over $15 million was spent by the federal government on welfare and relief, and an additional $6.4 million was spent on construction.[117] The New Deal enacted by Roosevelt and the Seventy-third Congress was in many ways the final piece in the assembly of a unified city/county political apparatus. Services like street paving and sewer construction were expanded, while major building projects like John Gaston Hospital, Crump Stadium, and Riverside Drive transformed the landscape of Shelby County. During Roosevelt's first hundred days, Crump voted for every piece of New Deal legislation, including the National Recovery Act, the Agricultural Adjustment Act, and the Tennessee Valley Authority.

As the 1932 campaign season wound down, disgruntled citizens re-formed the Voters League to challenge the county organization outside the confines of the Democratic Party. Seventy members, including Malcolm Patterson, met in October to outline their platform. President John M. Dean explained: "We are against machine rule from whatever source it emanates. We shall strive to wrest our government agencies from the hands of a one-man power and restore them to the people."[118] Notwithstanding their enthusiasm, there was even less hope of wrestling Shelby County from the Crump apparatus than the year before. However, six weeks after their reestablishment, funds went missing from the city treasury. The resulting scandal threatened to disrupt the political landscape of Shelby County and gave the anti-Crump forces their best chance to weaken the Democratic machine.

In the early evening of December 15, city treasurer J. H. Hessen left $1,774 unattended on his desk while he visited the mayor. When he returned to his office, the money was gone. According to Hessen, the only person in the office when he came back was finance commissioner A. P. "Tony" Walsh.[119] The generalissimos, aware of the political implications, reacted swiftly. Mayor Overton and the commission hired the accounting firm of Homer K. Jones to audit all city departments,[120] which revealed shortages amounting to over $52,000.[121] Perhaps the most shocking discovery was that Walsh had borrowed $6,648 from the treasury, leaving an IOU in its place.[122]

As the audit moved forward, Commissioner Walsh found himself in an untenable situation. Consequently, on the last day of 1932 Walsh submitted his resignation to the mayor. The resignation was accepted at a special meeting of the commission,[123] and a few weeks later the Shelby County grand jury indicted the chief bookkeeper of the streets department, M. D. Sabin, for embezzlement.[124] The newspapers gleefully commented on the administration's travails. For example, the *Evening Appeal* referred to the scandal as "the city haul,"[125] and claimed the "Shelby County political machine is breaking up."[126] Without a clear explanation of the shortages, rumor replaced fact. One held that Crump had long been aware of the scandal but did not allow Overton to weed out the corruption.[127]

In an attempt to quell the growing criticism, Mayor Overton disclosed over local radio all that was known of the shortages in early

February 1933. The mayor reported that, in addition to the $1,774 in cash, $36,000 was missing from the city engineering department, over $3,000 paid to the city had not been credited to its account, and financial records had been altered to cover up a $4,276.73 deficit for 1929.[128] Meanwhile in Washington, Crump grew alarmed at the slow pace of the investigation. The congressman pleaded with Overton and Attorney General McLain to indict Hessen and Walsh.[129] When indictments were not forthcoming, Crump exploded: "The public does not understand the city officials' dilatoriness in placing responsibility of the shortage, and I am frank to say I am one of them—I cannot understand, for it is all to me so very plain."[130]

Overton assured Crump that they wanted desperately to act but "to attempt an indictment and fail, or to get an indictment and then not have proof to sustain it, would put us all in a bad light."[131] In early May Crump gathered with the generalissimos in Louisville, Kentucky, to watch the Kentucky Derby and discuss how to handle the political crisis in Memphis.[132] The details of their discussion are not known, but six days after the conference, Hessen and Walsh were indicted on embezzlement charges.[133]

Sabin was the first to go on trial but the proceedings afforded no details because the former clerk pled guilty. The court promptly sentenced him to six years in prison.[134] Hessen and Walsh went on trial in July, but both defendants were found not guilty.[135] Although Walsh and Hessen were not convicted, the imprisonment of Sabin offered proof that graft would not be tolerated. The question remained, however, whether the city hall scandal would permanently damage the organization.

The Voters League hoped to exploit this situation, but the membership could not decide what to do. Some wanted to challenge the machine directly while others wished only to promote honest elections and increase citizen involvement in politics. In March, the more activist-minded members introduced a resolution which demanded the ouster of the city commission, but the measure was defeated by the executive committee of the league.[136] Two months later former league president John M. Dean and his successor, John W. McCall, resigned in protest over criticism of the Shelby County organization.[137] Their resignation meant that the moderate wing of the league was gone, and the remaining members launched a widespread investigation of city government.

Crump publicly dismissed the group, stating to the press: "I don't know a thing in the world about the Voters League.... [I]t'll vanish into thin air before the next election and accomplish nothing."[138] The congressman's casual dismissal masked the fact that he knew a great deal about the league because the generalissimos kept him informed of their activities. The nervousness felt by the machine leadership was shared by others on the receiving end of the league's curiosity. When league member Ben W. Kohn began investigating the possible link between gambling interests and the Democratic regulars, he was severely beaten by a nightclub bouncer.[139] Although there is no evidence Crump had anything to do with the incident, he was pleased that it happened: "How I did read and reread that story where Ben Kohn was hit in the jaw, and he in turn hit the concrete."[140] The attack on Kohn dampened the ardor of the league, but they seethed with anger and still hoped somehow to destroy the Shelby organization.

Crump must have been deeply troubled as he observed from Washington the scandals and recriminations weakening his carefully constructed political structure. Service in Congress, while sometimes frustrating, afforded him some national prestige and improved Memphis's position in obtaining federal funds. On the other hand his influence in Washington was predicated on a politically stable Memphis. Crump knew full well the only thing that stood between his organization and political oblivion was one electoral defeat. As 1933 ended, Crump carefully considered his future and came to a decision. It was time to go home.

"The Honor of Having
No Opposition"

In March 1934 Crump announced that he was leaving the House of Representatives at the end of the year.[1] The congressman claimed his business interests could no longer stand his absence, but the damage done to the organization's prestige and his disappointment in not playing a larger national role both played significant parts in his decision. Not wanting to leave the field open for rival candidates, the organization announced the following day that city attorney Walter Chandler was slated as Crump's replacement.[2] A World War I veteran and former state senator, Chandler was a loyal member of the organization, but not a member of the inner circle. While the generalissimos were pleased to learn Crump was coming home, at least one was unsure of Chandler's abilities. "Chandler is a good lawyer, but, frankly, he is not much help . . . in directing the policy of the city," commented Attorney General McLain.[3] Nevertheless, Crump wanted someone with impeccable credentials, which Chandler had.

When the announcement was made, officials in Washington expressed regret over Crump's decision. Secretary of State Cordell Hull lamented his departure from the nation's capital: "I know of no other member during the past years who within so brief a time . . . has impressed his ability to a greater extent upon his colleagues than yourself."[4] Speaking at Nashville, Postmaster General James Farley praised Crump for his "steadfast support" of the president's policies and bemoaned his leaving the House of Representatives.[5] President Roosevelt, however, said nothing.

Back in Memphis, organization leaders were worried over possible effects of the recent financial scandal on voter confidence. Citizens were canvassed and it was determined that there was very little opposition to the administration.[6] Since there was concern that the Voters League might upset the machine's firm hold on Shelby County, several operatives were ordered by Rice and McLain to infiltrate their ranks.[7] One such operative, county truant officer Ed Pass, had dinner with attorney Ben Kohn, the organization's most vocal critic, where he learned the league's strategy for the upcoming campaign. Two pieces of information were of greatest concern to the leadership. First, it was clear from Kohn's conversation that the Voters League planned to support independent Democrat Lewis Pope in his bid to unseat Governor McAlister, and secondly, they had approached county register Ben James to run on their ticket.[8]

A former member of the anti-Crump bloc, James had joined the organization in 1926 when he was selected to run for register.[9] James was rather popular among county voters and apparently felt he owed little allegiance to the organization. This, combined with the tactics used by the Voters League, gave the generalissimos cause for concern. At the same time James's loyalty came under suspicion, Crump decided to add a labor leader to the August slate because "with all the things that Roosevelt is doing for labor and working people, by rights Labor is entitled to one of those county offices."[10] Consequently, the decision was made to withdraw support for James's reelection. In his place the organization chose Jake Cohen, president of the Trades and Labor Council. Unwilling to accept the decision, James took the Voters League's offer of support and ran against Cohen.

The endorsement of Pope and James by the Voters League halted their slide toward political oblivion. It also forced Crump and the generalissimos to take the August elections more seriously. Crump was weary and did not have much faith in McAlister, but he was left with no choice but to fight hard against Pope.[11] The governor's lackadaisical attitude towards his reelection was but one problem facing the county organization in the summer of 1934. Of grave concern were reports that Cohen's candidacy made many Shelby County voters uneasy because he was a foreign-born Jew and labor activist.[12] The Voters League exploited this sentiment as James canvassed voters across the county.[13]

To combat the League's offensive against Cohen, Crump wrote several foreign embassies asking for "an authentic list of American citizens, of foreign birth, who have . . . distinguished themselves in the United States. . . ."[14] With the information gleaned from foreign dignitaries, the organization compiled a list of distinguished naturalized Americans which they used in campaign advertisements.[15] Rice then ordered all candidates and ward captains to contact every voter in their district and urge them to vote for Cohen.[16] In addition to countering the charges against Cohen, ward rallies were held throughout the county in support of all machine candidates. Five thousand people listened to Mayor Overton, Commissioner Davis, and others speak at South Side Park, while impromptu speeches by organization workers were held on six downtown street corners.[17]

Due to the diligence of ward captains, 35,000 citizens paid their poll taxes, which increased the number of qualified voters in Shelby County to 60,000.[18] The efficiency of the machine could not be overcome by the alliance between the Voters League, Ben James, and Lewis Pope. Fifty thousand votes were cast, with 31,241 given to Cohen in contrast to James's 8,234.[19] In addition to county successes, the machine racked up impressive totals in the Democratic primary. McAlister received 27,776 ballots, while Pope got only 2,757.[20] The defeat of James and Pope signaled the demise of the Voters League. Like the Ku Klux Klan and Rowlett Paine before them, the Voters League was crushed beneath the electoral juggernaut of the Shelby County organization. It would be several years before another credible threat emerged to challenge Crump in Shelby County.

As we have seen, one of Crump's longstanding goals was to develop a publicly owned utility for the citizens of Memphis. The creation of the Tennessee Valley Authority in May 1933 provided the organization with a mechanism to bring this about. TVA directors agreed to erect transmission lines to Memphis if the city constructed a plant to distribute the electricity. A referendum was required to issue bonds to begin construction, which was held in November 1934. The organization employed its usual efforts of rallies and voter canvassing to insure a large turnout, which insured an unprecedented victory. The number of citizens voting for the measure was 32,735, which was a validation of Crump's opposition to privately owned utilities.[21]

Although the 1934 elections destroyed the last vestiges of opposition to Crump's leadership, another weakness became apparent when the former congressman returned home at the end of the year. In January 1935, *Collier's* magazine published an article entitled "Sinners in Dixie," which surveyed criminal activities in Tennessee, Mississippi, and Arkansas. As the biggest city in the Mid-South, Memphis received the most attention.[22]

The author, Owen P. White, traveled to Memphis in the fall of 1934 under the guise of studying soil erosion,[23] but in reality was studying the erosion of law and order in the Bluff City. A nightclub brawl and other illegal activities were witnessed by the author as he investigated the growth of organized crime in Memphis. White concluded that vice flourished because the people wanted to participate in illegal activities while local politicians received campaign contributions from criminal leaders; ". . . it is upon commercialized vice that the burden of paying its overhead has been placed by Congressman Crump's political organization, which runs Shelby County."[24]

"Another popular method whereby the citizens of Memphis contribute to the pampered upkeep of their politicians and gamblers is for them to play policy," wrote the correspondent for *Collier's*. Policy was an illegal lottery where players purchased a number that gave them a chance to win a large sum of money.

The article mentioned other southern cities, most notably Little Rock, but Memphians felt they had been singled out for extra condemnation. The *Memphis Commercial Appeal* editorialized that *Collier's* should apologize for being "unfair,"[25] while a staff writer for the *Memphis Press-Scimitar* argued that the "big shots who came to Memphis found booze because they looked for it. . . . They found what they were looking for—just as they can find it anywhere in this country."[26]

Yet as the *Collier's* article suggested, Memphis had a culture of crime that was hard to uproot.[27] For example, the notorious gangster George Barnes, alias "Machine Gun Kelly," hailed from Memphis and was captured there in 1933.[28] Not even the local correctional institution was free of vice; a moonshine still, several thousand gallons of mash, and fifteen gallons of whisky were discovered at the county penal farm in 1935.[29] According to the FBI, Memphis had a higher crime rate than New York City.[30]

The most damaging figures came from the statistician for the Prudential Insurance Company, Dr. Frederick L. Hoffman, who claimed Memphis was the murder capital of the United States.[31] City officials countered that Hoffman's figures were unfair because they did not take into account violent encounters in the countryside which led to victims being taken to Memphis hospitals. "If a man gets shot at Blytheville [Arkansas] and dies in a Memphis hospital, we're charged up with another murder," said police chief Will Lee.[32] Despite the anger of some Memphians, the *Collier's* author was essentially correct in his analysis of the relationship between crime and politics. Crump and his stalwarts always balanced the desires of the voters with the need to protect and expand the organization's power. Looking realistically at the situation, it must not have been hard for machine leaders to determine that Memphians were anxious to engage in certain illegal activities. Therefore, Crump had to walk a fine line between supporting law enforcement and recreational sin if he wanted his political organization to stay in power. The same week *Collier's* appeared on Memphis newsstands, police moved against several criminal enterprises. Arrests were made for possession of illegal liquor, gambling, and policy writing.[33] Because large amounts of cash were available to gangsters for posting bond, procedures were changed allowing only property to be used for bail.[34] This made it harder for alleged criminals to flee and forfeit their bond.

Although all vice activities were targeted, the policy racket received the lion's share of attention. The police department was intimately familiar with the policy racket; one runner even sold numbers in the police station.[35] It was estimated that in Memphis, policy employed two thousand people who handled fifteen thousand bets daily. Paying usually no more than fifteen cents, a player selected three numbers between one and seventy-eight. If one of their numbers was among the twelve drawn, they won a certain amount of money.[36] In order to put a "lid" on the racket, police systematically raided policy establishments, confounding the underworld and press alike. The *Commercial Appeal* asked, "Why these 'lids' on vice and crime? Why are they opened now, then closed, then opened again?"[37] Echoing the newspaper, gangland leaders vowed they would be "back making our rounds again soon."[38]

Memphians were used to frequent raids against organized crime that ended once publicity was garnered. It was expected by all concerned that policy games would reopen as soon as public interest waned. But city leaders were determined to eradicate gambling and restore confidence in law enforcement. Racketeers like Nollo Grandi, owner of the Red Onion Club, pleaded with city officials for permission to begin again,[39] but the answer given was "You're shutdown— for good."[40] Officers were also warned "not to tolerate policy houses on your beats if you value your jobs."[41]

The fines for running a policy game were also increased by city court, to "take the profit out of policy writing," according to one judge;[42] while the middle class joined administration efforts to crush gambling. A minister and attorney gathered information on policy writers,[43] while a Parent-Teacher Association complaint ended the practice of merchants using pinball machines as gaming devices.[44] Meanwhile raids continued through the summer, spreading to include prostitution. Notorious madams like "Dutch Mary" Sherron were arrested for running disorderly houses, while individual prostitutes were detained for vagrancy.[45]

Crump and his lieutenants apparently decided it was time to sever their alliance with gangsters. In order to end this relationship, much depended on the police. In years past, organization leaders were restricted from attacking gangland crime because of limited controls over law enforcement. Civil service protection had been afforded the Memphis police in 1910, making it difficult to remove officers from the force.

Shelby County legislators pushed through the Tennessee General Assembly an omnibus bill which included the elimination of civil service protection for Memphis police.[46] Before the bill passed in February, an officer suspected of wrongdoing was entitled to a trial by his superiors with the right to appeal their decision to the city commission and the courts.[47] The new "merit" law gave the police commissioner authority to dismiss officers at will, without the right of an appeal by the employee.[48] Individual officers were described as "frightened" and "jumpy" as they made their rounds,[49] while machine leaders kept a watchful eye.

In conjunction with the establishment of the "merit system," officers were transferred, while others were demoted or forced to retire.[50] The abolition of civil service thwarted gangsters' attempts to purchase cooperation from the police while at the same time further politicizing the operation of law enforcement. No doubt any policeman who dared support a political candidate not chosen by the machine quickly found himself unemployed. However, it is also true that the ending of the policy racket was in large part due to the merit system.

As the drive against organized crime got under way, it was discovered that the city court clerk was returning fines to those who had been found guilty of violating the state liquor law. Although the United States had abandoned prohibition in 1933, the state of Tennessee had not. Mayor Overton forced the resignation of city court clerk W. L. Clark in spite of objections from city court judge Lewis T. Fitzhugh. Revealing that he had ordered Clark to remit the fines, Fitzhugh vowed to continue the practice whenever "a mistake of judgment has been made."[51]

Fitzhugh had enjoyed organization support since 1927, but that ended when Overton accused the judge of keeping the fines for himself rather than returning them.[52] Describing the situation as a "racket," Overton vowed to drive "out crookedness in the city government."[53] Fitzhugh countered that every Memphian knew "there is a corrupt alliance between ... the political machine and the criminal classes," and by attacking him they were diverting attention from this fact.[54] The judge also argued that the organization wanted to replace him with someone who would cooperate more fully in the law enforcement drive.

In response to Mayor Overton's accusations, the Shelby County grand jury indicted Fitzhugh and Clark for larceny and receiving stolen property. Fitzhugh lashed out by stating he was being "railroaded through a controlled grand jury upon perjured evidence

procured by this conscienceless machine."[55] This statement landed Fitzhugh in jail when criminal court judge Phil H. Wallace had him arrested for contempt of court. After posting a $250 bond, Fitzhugh proclaimed to a packed courtroom: "Conscious of the rectitude of my official conduct, and confident, therefore, of absolute vindication, I will retire temporarily from the bench...."[56] A guilty verdict was handed down in Fitzhugh's contempt trial despite his argument that he meant no disrespect to the courts.[57]

Attorney general W. Tyler McLain and city attorney Will Gerber argued at Fitzhugh's larceny trial that the former judge had stolen thirty-two thousand dollars of forfeited fees. Ledger books where fees were recorded, along with witnesses who did not receive their remitted fines, were introduced into evidence, while the defense argued no money had been found in Fitzhugh's possession.[58] The jury deliberated for over forty hours before reporting they were deadlocked nine to three for Fitzhugh's acquittal. With no choice left to him, the presiding judge declared a mistrial.[59] Attorney General McLain vowed to try Fitzhugh again, but the former judge died less than a year later.[60]

The Fitzhugh trial, while on the surface a defeat for the organization, did help in its war on the underworld. According to one newspaper account, bootleggers attributed the fate of Judge Fitzhugh to the police department's zeal.[61] No doubt many officers felt the need to be more diligent and honest due to the fall of Judge Fitzhugh as well as the implementation of the merit system.

But what of Lewis Fitzhugh; was he a crooked judge? According to evidence discussed in the newspaper accounts, it is possible that Fitzhugh was targeted for removal only after he refused to cease remitting liquor fines. The organization leadership was certainly not above creating scapegoats to deflect attention from the appalling crime rate. Apparently they chose court clerk W. L. Clark for that role, and, when Fitzhugh stood by him, he was targeted as well.

No doubt Crump and his stalwarts wanted the message sent to the city bureaucracy that the crackdown on the underworld was real, and perhaps they chose the fine-remitting practice to send the directive that they were indeed serious. Had Fitzhugh stayed out of the controversy surrounding Clark's dismissal, he perhaps would have remained on the bench. Given that Attorney General McLain was a member of the Crump inner circle, it is not hard to imagine the Shelby County grand jury being influenced by the machine to indict Fitzhugh in order to eliminate a recalcitrant official.

The offensive directed at the underworld, as already stated, was successful in crushing the policy racket while curbing other forms of gambling. One area of crime that was more difficult to address was homicide. In 1934, for example, ninety-three Memphians were murdered.[62] The majority were killed with pistols, although eight were killed with shotguns, twenty with knives, and five were clubbed to death.[63] As we have seen, the Overton administration vehemently argued that Memphis was unfairly labeled the "murder capital" of the nation, but, as the number of deaths continued to rise from year to year,[64] it became more difficult to combat that image.

In January 1935, just before "Sinners in Dixie" appeared in *Collier's*, Overton began carefully scrutinizing police reports for ways to curb the homicide rate. Writing to police commissioner Davis, Overton stated, "I think by making a very careful analysis of these places we can find out the cause of these homicides and correct the conditions which are causing them." The mayor then chided the homicide bureau for not making a more detailed investigation.[65]

Chief inspector W. T. Griffin suggested to the mayor that adding a bureau of ballistics would "add to the effectiveness of prosecutions of homicide cases."[66] But to Overton, Griffin was missing the point. The mayor was amenable to the idea of a ballistics department, but he wrote that "prosecution of these cases is much better at present than our efforts to analyze the causes of our high homicide rate. . . ."[67]

The white middle classes strongly supported Crump's progressive reforms as evidenced by this 1913 George W. Curtis cartoon. Courtesy Memphis Public Library and Information Center.

In 1914 classes were held to insure voters correctly spelled the name of Crump stalwart John Reichman, candidate for Shelby County Sheriff. Courtesy Memphis Public Library and Information Center.

Crump's middle class support plummeted in the wake of his removal from the mayor's office as seen in this cartoon by Pulitzer Prize–winner J. P. Alley, *Memphis Commercial Appeal*, February 10, 1916. Courtesy Memphis Public Library and Information Center.

Crump with children at the Memphis Fairgrounds, 1935. "Generalissimo" Frank Rice is on the far right next to Crump. Courtesy Memphis Public Library and Information Center.

Crump around the time of his election to the U.S. Congress in 1930. Courtesy Memphis Public Library and Information Center.

Crump shortly after resigning the mayor's office in 1940. Courtesy Memphis Public Library and Information Center.

Organization candidates slated for the 1938 Democratic Primary. Courtesy Memphis Public Library and Information Center.

Shelby County Attorney General W. Tyler McLain in 1938.
Courtesy Memphis Public Library and Information Center.

Mayor Watkins Overton at the inauguration of air mail service to Memphis, June 15, 1931. Courtesy Memphis Public Library and Information Center.

Frank Rice managed Crump's first political campaigns and remained one of his most trusted advisors until his death in 1938. Courtesy Memphis Public Library and Information Center.

Overton was no doubt sincere in his desire to root out the causes of murder, which helps to explain even further the 1935 underworld crackdown. But it was a difficult problem to solve, involving much more than shutting down a criminal enterprise. Despite the zealousness with which the city attacked organized crime, the murder rate soared to 103 deaths in 1935.[68]

Homicide reports forwarded to the mayor revealed the depths of the culture of violence in Memphis. Most of the murders resulted not from premeditation, but rather were crimes of passion committed without much thought. An angry confrontation, exacerbated by liquor, was the standard reason Memphians turned to violence. For example, in 1937, an inebriated laborer came home and crawled into bed fully clothed with his common-law wife. She insisted he take his clothes off and in response he got out of bed, grabbed a shovel, and beat the woman to death.[69] In a similar vein, a man was stabbed to death after attempting to stop an argument between a drunken common-law husband and wife.[70]

It was obvious to the Crump machine that vice contributed to the appalling murder rate. Through the rest of the decade the police continued to exert pressure on the criminal element; dice games were broken up,[71] and businesses were investigated for possible liquor violations.[72] The homicide rate, however, remained an intractable problem.

In the midst of Crump's war on crime, Overton and the city commission faced reelection. How deeply the Voters League was buried can be measured in that no candidate rose to challenge the administration. The organization held no rallies, nor was there any concerted effort to register voters. This nonchalant attitude extended to election day when, instead of campaigning, the mayor and commission spent the day considering bids for construction projects financed by the federal Public Works Administration. The election was marked by the lowest voter turnout in a decade; only

11,086 ballots were marked for Overton and the commission.[73] Reflecting on this, Overton declared: "We all appreciated the honor of having no opposition."[74]

As we have seen, Crump's relationship with the president was strained due to Crump's disappointment in not playing a larger role in the 1932 campaign. However, the situation between these two powerful leaders improved when Crump was appointed to the Democratic National Committee in 1936. The Memphis leader exerted newfound influence when he hand-picked the secretary of the national campaign committee.[75] Crump publicly supported the president's reelection bid, going so far as to resign from the Mortgage Bankers Association when they attacked Roosevelt during a convention in Memphis.[76] In September Crump joined the president on a tour of the Smoky Mountains, where Roosevelt gently teased Crump about a recently built city kennel paid for with federal funds: "Well, Ed, what about that dog house down in Memphis?" Crump replied: "Oh, the dog house is fine. It will mean a lot of votes for you down there."[77]

During the campaign Crump kept in close touch with Roosevelt campaign manager Farley.[78] Recognizing the importance of the African American vote in Tennessee, Farley asked Crump to name "the outstanding colored man in your state" to serve on a campaign committee.[79] Because of Crump's alliance with African American Memphians, Tennessee blacks were, to some extent at least, represented at the highest levels of the Democratic Party.[80]

Crump also phoned Farley to suggest that the president should strongly emphasize how much economic progress had been made under his leadership. Specifically, he wanted Roosevelt to mention improvements made in banking, securities, and railroad transportation. In a letter to Roosevelt, Farley outlined Crump's ideas and strongly endorsed them: "I honestly feel, Mr. President, that there is a great deal of merit to these thoughts which Mr. Crump has passed along to me."[81] In an address delivered in Chicago seven days after Farley's letter was written, Roosevelt incorporated many of Crump's suggestions in the form of rhetorical questions: "Do you have a deposit in a bank? It is safer today than it has ever been in our history. . . . Are you an investor? Your stocks and bonds are up to five- and six-year high levels. . . . Are you in railroads? Freight loadings are steadily going up."[82] Crump was pleased and the two grew closer as a result.[83]

Back in Memphis ward captains were appointed to register voters, assure their presence at the polls, and raise campaign funds. The majority of ward captains and lieutenants were city and county employees whose job no doubt depended, at least in part, on how successfully their ward turned out on election day.[84] Voter lists were distributed to ward leaders which included not only the citizens' phone numbers but also voting precinct and religious affiliation.[85] Captains and lieutenants surveyed citizens by phone, asking who they planned to vote for. These preferences were then recorded and reported back to Crump. Many voters were described as "friendly" while others were referred to as "unfriendly and vicious."[86] Thousands of dollars collected from individuals, businesses, and government employees were turned over to Mayor Overton for dispersal.[87] For example, the employees of the street-cleaning department contributed $314 to the organization's coffers.[88] Money gathered in Shelby County was turned over to the state finance committee, which collected $90,000 from across Tennessee. Sixty-five thousand dollars was sent to Roosevelt's campaign, while $25,000 remained in Tennessee to finance the state campaign.[89]

In addition to the personal touch, the organization broadcast radio advertisements that extolled the president's accomplishments:

They said Fulton will surely fail
to run a boat without a sail.

But he did it.
They said Roosevelt is off the track
his New Deal cannot bring us back.
But he did it.
Join a grateful nation in returning
a great president to the presidency.
Vote for Franklin Delano Roosevelt
and the entire Democratic ticket on
Tuesday November 3rd.[90]

The voters of Shelby County cast 61,883 ballots for Roosevelt, while only 2,149 voted for his Republican opponent, Alfred M. Landon.[91] Roosevelt's victory signaled a new era in American politics. African Americans, farmers, industrial workers, and progressives transformed the Democratic Party into a broad multi-interest coalition.[92]

The significance of a biracial, multiethnic faction in the midst of the segregated South was not lost on the national Democratic Party. As the correspondence between Crump and Farley suggests, Democrats made note of the Memphis leader's alliance with African American voters and used this knowledge to recast their party in 1936. This was even more apparent with Roosevelt's bid for a third presidential term in 1940. The national party recruited Shelby County Colored Democratic Club chairman Dr. J. E. Walker for a speaking tour of Illinois on behalf of the Roosevelt ticket. While there, Walker spoke to thousands at several rallies, participated in a radio broadcast with former Indiana governor Paul McNutt, and discussed strategy with Interior Secretary Harold Ickes.[93] Applying Crump's techniques on a national scale, Roosevelt and Farley brought large numbers of African Americans to the Democratic fold, altering the American political landscape for decades to come.

With his attention focused on the presidential contest, Crump was little interested in the Tennessee governor's race. It will be recalled that Crump reluctantly endorsed incumbent Hill McAlister in 1934, but the following year their political marriage came to an end when the governor introduced legislation to create a state sales tax. Crump vociferously opposed the measure, calling McAlister "our sorriest governor" for introducing it. As with other measures opposed by Crump, the Shelby delegation successfully prevented the bill from becoming law.[94] Faced with the withdrawal of Crump's patronage, McAlister announced he would not run for a third term. Tennessee congressman Gordon Browning and McAlister's 1934 campaign manager, Burgin Dossett, both vied for the Democratic nomination, but Crump refused to endorse either one.

The situation became more complicated when Crump's old ally McKellar endorsed Dossett for fear Browning would run against him as he had in 1934.[95] The senator tried to convince Crump to support his candidate, but the Memphis leader demurred. In an attempt to gauge public opinion, the generalissimos sent operatives across the state to survey the two campaigns.[96] According to one report, "[T]he consensus of opinion is that if Mr. Crump does not take a hand, McKellar will take the credit for electing the governor, although the opinion is that Shelby can elect the next governor."[97]

Faced with this possible loss of prestige, Crump endorsed Browning in mid-July. The two men had served in Washington together and Crump emphasized that point when the announcement was made. Meanwhile, McKellar quietly backed away from Dossett.[98] Despite this minor rift between Crump and McKellar, the two remained close allies. Although Browning appeared the more formidable candidate, Crump's endorsement was critical to his success. In the August primary Browning received 60,000 votes in Shelby County, while Dossett was held to a mere 825. Across Tennessee voters gave Browning one of the largest margins of victory in state history—243,463 to Dossett's 109,170.[99] Crump's support of Browning paid off in ways he could not have predicted. Most notably, *Time* magazine covered the primary and marveled at Crump's electoral success. *Time's* correspondent even went so far as to describe Crump as "one of the South's most remarkable politicians."[100] No doubt the Shelby County leader reveled in this coverage. However, the appearance in *Time*, combined with his higher status within the national Democratic Party, may have inflated Crump's ego to such a degree that it endangered the efficiency of his finely tuned political apparatus.

This situation came into sharper focus when the Mississippi River Valley flooded in January 1937. Cresting at 48.67 feet, floodwaters damaged homes and farms throughout the Mid-South region.[101] Tributaries of the Mississippi, the Wolf River and Nonconnah Creek, flooded parts of North and South Memphis, causing $1,250,000 worth of damage.[102] When refugees from throughout the Mid-South poured into the city, Mayor Overton organized a massive relief effort. An emergency flood committee was formed which coordinated efforts with the American Red Cross, the federal Works Project Administration, and the Memphis Welfare Committee. The fairgrounds was converted into a camp for flood victims, but was quickly overwhelmed as the number climbed to over fifty thousand refugees. Makeshift shelters were established in schools and other public buildings, but overcrowding and poor sanitary conditions created a public health catastrophe.[103] To ease the burden of overcrowding, the emergency committee decided on January 28 to transport refugees out of Memphis into north Mississippi and western Tennessee.[104]

Crump, sick with the flu, left these details to Overton and his committee.[105] Upon his recovery the Memphis leader inspected the fairgrounds refugee camp and was outraged by what he saw. Unaware that Overton had already taken steps to relieve the situation, Crump fired off a strongly worded letter to the mayor: "It is criminal on our part to pack all of these people—men, women and children—like sardines in a box at the Fairgrounds."[106] Given how skillfully he had handled the crisis, Overton was understandably offended by Crump's harsh tone: "I do not think it was criminal to put the people in the Fairgrounds because there was no other place to put them. It would have been criminal to have kept them there. We didn't."[107] This was the first time Crump had ever seriously questioned Overton's abilities, but it would not be the last.

In South Memphis several important industrial areas were threatened by rising floodwaters, including the Gulf Refining Company and the Memphis Hardwood Flooring Company. When the operators of these businesses begged Crump for assistance,[108] he took personal charge of shoring up broken levees just as he had done in 1912.[109] The situation became so dire he ordered the police to conscript at gunpoint any African Americans found enjoying the entertainment on Beale Avenue to work on the levees.[110] Crump ordered city engineer William B. Fowler to oversee sandbagging at Nonconnah Creek. When Overton discovered Fowler was not at his assigned post, the mayor removed him as city engineer. Once the truth was discovered, Fowler was quickly rehired.[111] In the end, the city weathered the devastating flood rather well. Despite Crump's interference, Overton and his committee did an admirable job of tending to the refugees and broken levees. The mayor should have been celebrated for his handling of the crisis, but instead he was left with Crump's disapproval. As the floodwaters receded, the relationship between Overton and Crump was left broken in its wake.

A comprehensive flood control system had been a goal of Crump's since his mayoralty, and he saw an opportunity to fulfill this goal in the summer of 1937. Bills were submitted to congress by Chandler and McKellar, but they faced opposition from Roosevelt. The president wanted to limit flood control projects to the Ohio River basin, and he warned House flood control chairman W. M. Whittington that "if a single item affecting the Mississippi River was in the bill," he would veto it.[112] Through his former secretary Marvin Pope, who was in the nation's capital, Crump sent a message to several southern congressmen urging them to support the Memphis bill. Whittington, a representative from the Mississippi Delta, vowed to "do anything that Ed Crump wants" and was as good as his word. Nine million dollars was allocated for flood control at Memphis, but to assuage the president, work was delayed until 1938.[113] Although Crump did not contact the president directly, he nevertheless played a significant role in bringing flood control to Memphis through his influence with other southern leaders. When the project was completed, Memphis was spared any further flood damage from the unpredictable Mississippi.

The Shelby County organization emerged from the river disaster and the struggle in Washington for flood control measures relatively unscathed. To most political observers the machine was as secure as ever, but the tattered relationship between Crump and Overton had weakened its structure. As this deterioration was taking place, another crisis loomed in Nashville. The ensuing strife tested whether or not the organization could withstand another battle with a Tennessee executive.

"God Bless You, Boss"

Although Crump had supported Gordon Browning for governor in 1936, the two leaders barely trusted one another. Crump became suspicious when the governor began to associate with former allies of his nemesis Luke Lea. His skepticism increased after Browning appointed anti-Crump Democrat Lewis Pope to head a special investigation of the state's back taxes office.[1] These actions suggested to Crump that Browning might form a coalition that would exclude him from state affairs. For his part, the governor expected at any moment to be treated disrespectfully by the Shelby County leader.

Each man's suspicion of the other weighed heavily on them both, although the two were cordial in the early months of 1937.[2] During the regular session of the general assembly the Shelby delegation supported Browning's legislative agenda with little opposition.[3] In July Overton and Hale met with Browning in Nashville where they discussed highway maintenance and state jobs for Shelby County residents. The governor was wary of the two generalissimos, but the meeting ended amicably.[4] Nevertheless, Browning continued to doubt Crump. The situation grew worse when Tennessee's junior senator, Nathan Bachman, unexpectedly died. It fell to Browning to appoint a replacement, and he chose labor union president George L. Berry.[5]

Before the decision was announced, Memphis attorney Abe Waldauer, who served with Browning during World War I, visited the governor and urged him to appoint Crump. When the Memphis leader learned of this he ordered Waldauer to call Browning and tell him he was not interested and "to forget it."[6] Despite this firm denial, Browning believed Crump really did want the appointment and was bitterly disappointed at being passed over.

Secure in this erroneous assumption, Browning came to Memphis in September. Meeting with Crump, the governor made an extraordinary offer. In exchange for Crump's endorsement of Browning for Berry's Senate seat in 1938, the governor promised to support Crump for the Senate in 1940, the year McKellar would be up for reelection. According to Crump, the governor boasted, "I can send you!"[7] Crump was deeply offended by Browning's attempt at a back-room deal. He not only objected to the suggestion that he would betray McKellar, but found the governor's callousness toward Berry intolerable. Perhaps more importantly, he was angered at Browning's suggestion that he had the power to send Crump back to Washington. After all, Crump, not Browning, was "one of the South's most remarkable politicians." As the meeting ended, the suspicions Crump harbored took form and became an impenetrable barrier between the two leaders.[8]

Apparently Browning sensed this as well, for when he returned to Nashville he laid plans to crush the Shelby County organization and its leader. On October 8 the governor called a special session of the general assembly to amend state election laws. Over a statewide radio broadcast Browning explained that he was trying to rid the state of a "tsar" who held "a deluge of corrupt ballots over the head of the state like a sword of Damocles."[9] With its obvious reference to Crump, Browning's speech was in effect a declaration of war against the Shelby County organization. The general assembly met on October 11 to debate the governor's plan to restrict the voting strength of

Tennessee's most populous counties. Browning's scheme gave each county a specific number of unit votes which were calculated based on the total votes cast within that county for the previous year's gubernatorial nominee divided by one hundred. As in the electoral college, the candidate that received the highest number of popular ballots was given the county's unit votes.[10] In effect, the measure would disenfranchise thousands of Tennessee voters.

Rural lawmakers, who strongly believed that the power of the state's urban centers should be curbed, supported the bill, while representatives of the four municipalities bitterly opposed the measure. Led by the Shelby delegation, urban representatives tried in vain to stop the bill's passage, but Browning's alliance with the rural bloc steamrolled over them. A mere nine days after the special session opened, the county unit bill became law. Emboldened by their success, rural lawmakers authorized the governor to investigate voter registration irregularities and purge allegedly fraudulent names from election books.[11] Both measures severely hamstrung the organization, and almost overnight Crump appeared to have lost nearly all his statewide influence.

But he refused to surrender to Browning and the rural legislators. Organization members filed suit in Davidson County Chancery Court, arguing that several lawmakers who voted for the county unit bill also held state jobs and therefore were barred from voting under the state's constitution. Surprisingly, they did not argue that the law violated Tennesseans' right to vote. It was perhaps a strange argument to make, but Crump and his lieutenants apparently did not believe they could win on constitutional grounds—yet they did. The Tennessee Supreme Court ruled in early 1938 that the county unit law was unconstitutional because it violated the Fourteenth Amendment.[12] The court's decision crippled Browning's offensive, but he looked to the 1938 Democratic primary to vindicate his position. The Crump organization intended to do the same.

A significant factor in the Shelby organization's favor was the level of public outrage over the county unit proposal. The governor apparently failed to grasp how deeply Tennesseans resented the law. Leading newspapers condemned the act while many citizens across the Volunteer State reacted in horror to the governor's attempt to restrict voting rights. As West Tennessee Republican J. Ross McKinney put it, "[E]very person in the State of Tennessee that is interested in free government should vigorously protest the enactment of this biased political proposal."[13] Even Tennesseans who normally despised Crump opposed the governor's position. The depth of voter anger gave Crump and his allies an important issue to exploit. The Memphis leader was confident that he and the anti-Browning forces "might lose a battle here and there, but I don't believe we will lose the war."[14] Before the battle could be joined, however, they needed a candidate.

In February 1938 Walter Chandler announced his candidacy for governor with the apparent support of Crump. However, it quickly became apparent that Chandler's candidacy was not well received because he was so closely identified with the Shelby organization. Bowing to the inevitable, Chandler withdrew his candidacy.[15] Prentice Cooper, a state senator from Shelbyville, announced he was seeking the Democratic nomination and Crump quickly endorsed him.[16] The organization threw itself into the campaign. Ward captains increased voter registration to 101,044,[17] while McKellar used his influence to control the state Democratic Executive Committee's appointment of county election boards across Tennessee.[18] Crump focused much of his attention on Cooper, sending him a list of points to make on the campaign trail: "I propose to fix it so Luke Lea will not have his long fingers around in the State's affairs. I will not bribe legislators to pass any kind of bill."[19]

While the organization focused all its attention on the gubernatorial race, an incident occurred between the Memphis police and the African American community which jeopardized their electoral chances far greater than anything Gordon Browning could do. In January 1938 the police received a report from a white woman who claimed that George W. Brooks, an African American postal worker, had "annoyed" her several times near the intersection of Iowa and Main streets in downtown Memphis.[20] Sensing a possible arrest, a trap was laid using the woman as bait. Detective A. O. Clark and another officer surprised Brooks as the woman entered his car, yelling, "This is the police." The woman leaped out of the car as Clark entered, brandishing his revolver. Sitting beside each other, Brooks and Clark exchanged fire. Brooks died instantly, having been shot "three or four times" at point-blank range.[21]

The account given by Clark left several questions unanswered, which eroded black confidence in the police. City officials simply accepted the department's version of what happened, but lingering doubts within the African American community led to protest. A committee of middle-class black leaders was formed during a mass meeting to seek redress from the city. First Baptist Church pastor T. O. Fuller, Blair T. Hunt, the principal of Booker T. Washington High School, J. E. Walker, president of Universal Life Insurance, and congregational pastor J. A. G. Grant met with Mayor Overton, but he failed to take action.[22]

By ignoring the complaint of the African American community, the organization gave strength to those blacks who felt the Crump organization should be abandoned. The newly formed Negro Independent Voters League, headed by salesman O. G. Sledge, argued that blacks did not receive enough from the organization to continue voting for their candidates.[23]

The callous way in which city hall dismissed police brutality complaints also angered the black community, leading some to openly support Browning's reelection. O. G. Sledge claimed the Negro Independent Voters League had four thousand members pledged to the governor.[24] Because there was concern that the black vote was in jeopardy, a swimming pool was opened in South Memphis and the administration promised a new park for the black community.[25]

The Democratic primary held on August 4, 1938, became a day of reckoning for Governor Browning. Tennesseans rejected the governor's ham-handed attempts at coercion by casting 238,000 votes for Cooper while a mere 150,000 ballots were marked for him. In Shelby County Browning received 9,000 votes to Cooper's 58,000, making Crump's revenge complete.[26]

There was, however, a discordant note played in the midst of victory. During the previous Democratic gubernatorial primary the organization's opponent received only 825 votes in Shelby County—but political conditions had since shifted. The cause of this turn apparently was the suspicious death of George W. Brooks. While race specific voting figures are not available, it is clear the disparity between the two elections was due to African Americans voting for Browning.[27] The outcome of the primary emboldened antiorganization sentiment within the African American community, and Crump decided to outmaneuver independently minded black voters.

The 1938 Democratic primary was the last election in which Crump's trusted generalissimos all played a part. Shortly before the August primary, Shelby County attorney general W. Tyler McLain died,[28] and in December Frank Rice also passed away.[29] Their deaths left a vacuum within the organization and severely restricted Crump's access to untrammeled political advice. Although the organization ran smoothly despite their deaths, Crump increasingly found himself surrounded by men who were afraid to offer unvarnished opinion. Without advisors willing to tell the truth, Crump was adrift in a sea of flattery. The isolation deepened as Crump's relationship with Overton deteriorated past the point of no return.

In previous years Crump and Overton had exchanged long letters where they discussed political and governmental affairs in a friendly

and equal tone. Overton freely offered advice, while Crump made suggestions rather than giving direct orders. In fact, Crump relied heavily on all of the generalissimos' counsel. This changed in 1938. The tone of their correspondence receded from affable and neighborly to curt and businesslike. Crump bombarded Overton with complaints about the poor condition of city streets and ordered their improvement.[30] The rift between Overton and Crump had a profound effect on the course of Memphis politics.

As we have seen, the city commission issued bonds in 1934 to construct an electric power plant to distribute TVA power in Memphis. The building was completed in 1937, but power lines and a distribution network were still needed to bring cheaper electricity to Shelby County consumers. Formed after the passage of the bond issue, the light and water commission recommended to Overton that the most cost-effective measure was to purchase the properties of the Memphis Power and Light Company.[31] Agreeing with this assessment, Overton authorized the light and water board to negotiate with the company in the summer of 1938. While the city board negotiated with Memphis Power and Light, Overton kept Crump informed of any details available to him,[32] and Crump was apparently satisfied to leave the negotiations in the hands of others. On September 30 Overton and the other parties announced the sale of the Memphis Power and Light Company's electrical distribution system to the city of Memphis for $13,500,000.[33] Overton and the light and water commissioners were congratulated for "having accomplished the greatest progressive step in our long and proud history."[34] Crump's name was never mentioned.

Given that Crump had struggled hard for decades to bring public power to Memphis, it was natural that his feelings would be bruised at having his contributions ignored. His subsequent actions however, went beyond attempting to heal his hurt feelings. Crump's personality had always contained a streak of arrogance, and this trait was magnified as he became a national celebrity. In the spring of 1938 *Collier's* magazine concluded in an in-depth profile that "Ed Crump can lift the telephone and with one command send sixty thousand sovereign Democrats to the secret polls to do his bidding."[35] This was at best an exaggeration, but Crump apparently came to believe his own legend.

Seething with jealousy, Crump determined to strike back against his old friend. Employing his loyalists on the city commission, Crump prevented adoption of the contract. The omission of the gas works in the contract was the reason given for the rejection, but Crump's wounded pride was the true motive.

From this point on he required his lieutenants to fawn over him rather than offer expert counsel. This is perhaps best seen in Clifford Davis's defense of Crump during the power deal controversy. Described as a "wise prophet" and "friend of the human race," Davis went on to say that "any commissioner could have made a pretty good mayor with Crump's help."[36] Davis also sniped at Overton, stating that the mayor had "blundered terribly" by ignoring Crump's counsel. Joining the attack, Crump snidely called Overton "little Jack Horner," who was "selfish" and "peeved."[37] Despite the invective, clearly it was Crump who was peeved and not the mayor.

In the wake of rejecting the agreement Crump met with the light and water commissioners and others, and they decided to renegotiate with Memphis Power and Light.[38] Even though he held no government post Crump conducted talks with the power company from November to February 1939. Despite their reluctance to negotiate, an agreement was reached, whereby the city was able to purchase the gas works in addition to the electrical distribution system. The only major difference between the Crump and Overton agreements was that the city did not purchase the company's steam-generating plant, opting instead to use its newly constructed facility.[39]

Before he became a national figure, Crump would never have done this to so loyal a friend, but celebrity got the better of him. In addition to his usurping the powers of the duly elected mayor of Memphis, his petulance nearly cost the city access to cheap electric power. Although the gas works were a fine addition, they were not imperative. The true goal, as Crump well knew, was electricity. Had either TVA or Memphis Power and Light balked at Crump's interference, Memphians would have lost the benefit of inexpensive electricity. It is thus difficult to escape the conclusion that in the late 1930s Crump was corrupted by fame. How much corruption had seeped into Crump's being can be gauged by his correspondence with one of the South's most noted journalists.

In the midst of the power company negotiations, North Carolina newspaper editor Jonathan Daniels wrote Crump asking for an interview. Daniels planned to write a series of articles on southern political leaders for the *Saturday Evening Post* and wanted to include the Memphis leader.[40] Inexplicably Crump refused to talk to Daniels, claiming he was too busy with the utilities matter to devote time to anything else.[41] In other words, he was far too important a man to give his attention to a mere journalist. Undeterred, the North Carolina editor traveled to Memphis in early December, where he interviewed several people and tried desperately to see Crump.[42] On December 8 Daniels visited Crump's office, but was again rebuffed.[43] Despite his inaccessibility, Crump chided Daniels for not being more persistent: "After my secretary wrote you that I was tied up, I am very sorry you didn't see fit to call at a later date."

Of greatest concern was that Daniels might include in his article a reference to Crump's relationship with famed blues composer W. C. Handy: "It has gone the rounds that Handy, a negro [*sic*] musician, played a conspicuous part in my first race for mayor. That is absolutely false. Handy came to my office, probably a year after I was mayor—said he had written a piece of music 'Beale Street Blues' and dedicated it to Mister Crump. Asked me to read it over and see if I could find any objections. I didn't object and he published it."[44] When Crump ran for mayor in 1909 it was common to have musicians play at rallies, and his campaign was no exception. According to Handy, he was hired by someone on Crump's staff to play at a meeting where he introduced a new composition entitled "Mr. Crump." During the campaign Crump's reform image was ridiculed by many African Americans who added derogatory lyrics to Handy's tune. After the race was over, Handy took those comments, added lyrics to his creation, and retitled it "The Memphis Blues": "Mr. Crump won't 'low no easy riders here ... We don't care what Mr. Crump don't 'low. We gon' to bar'l-house anyhow. Mr. Crump can go and catch hisself some air!"[45]

In 1913 Handy republished the song with lyrics that did not mention Crump at all. Given that Handy's "Beale Street Blues" was not composed until 1917, Crump was undoubtedly referring to the revised "Memphis Blues" in his letter to Daniels. Despite his wishes, Crump remained a popular subject for musicians. In 1927 the Beale Street Shieks (Frank Stokes and Dan Sane) recorded a song entitled "Mr. Crump Don't Like It," which was a variation on Handy's original lyrics.[46] During the 1937 flood a street singer was heard exclaiming: "Oh, the river's up and cotton's down, Mister Ed Crump, he runs this town...."[47]

When Daniels finished the article he sent a copy to Crump, who read the manuscript and demanded certain changes. He specifically objected to a quote he denied ever uttering: "Most people don't know anything at all about how to vote.... If you put Judas Iscariot on the ballot, he'd get a thousand votes in Shelby County."[48] More in keeping with his inflated ego, however, was his feeling that "the people of Memphis and throughout Tennessee have given me credit for many things which Mr. Daniels omitted entirely."[49] Despite his pleas, the requested changes were never made.[50] Daniels's piece added to

Crump's legend far more than it detracted from it, and it also accurately captured Crump's irritable nature: "The same man who can and does sometimes present an almost incoherent, gesticulatory anger to reporters and politicians can also be the pleasantest gentleman alive."[51]

By mid-1939 Crump had achieved two of his long-standing goals for Memphis—namely flood control and a publicly owned electrical utility. But one ambition remained unfulfilled—ending prohibition in Tennessee. When the general assembly convened in early 1939, Representative Lon Austin of Lexington introduced a bill giving counties the option to sell liquor, which would end Tennessee's thirty-year experiment in prohibition. Guiding the bill through the house was Memphis representative Charles Brown, suggesting that the machine was in part responsible for the bill's introduction. The proposal wound its way through the house and senate with little opposition.[52]

Governor Cooper vetoed the measure, reasoning that the "bill does not conform to my platform pledge made to the people of this state." When the governor's veto was overridden, Tennessee became the forty-fifth state in the union to allow the sale of liquor within its borders.[53] In vetoing the measure, Cooper was able to appear independent of the Memphis boss while keeping ties to antimachine prohibitionists. It was likely Crump acquiesced in the governor's action because support for the bill was stronger than Cooper's objection. Despite this disagreement, Crump and Cooper remained on very friendly terms.[54]

The local option law required a county to hold a referendum before liquor could be legally obtained. Shelby voters went to the polls in May and overwhelmingly voted for the legalizing of alcohol.[55] Selling liquor legally gave city and county governments the power to regulate the industry, ostensibly replacing gangsters with law-abiding merchants. The new law also brought in needed revenue for public services; $10,883 was added to government coffers in the first month after the end of prohibition.[56] As Memphians bought liquor from government-sanctioned dealers, what was left of the underworld saw its major cash business evaporate, which further dissipated organized crime in Memphis.

With the adoption of the local option measure, Crump's vision for Memphis was complete, but it came at a high cost. The once-strong partnership between the Memphis leader and Watkins Overton lay shattered in the wake of Crump's handling of the power-and-light agreement. The two ceased communicating with each other while Overton quietly laid plans to challenge the organization in the fall municipal contest. He was aware that Crump had no plans to slate him for a fourth term, so he hoped to run as an independent candidate. Working with his ally Commissioner Ralph Picard, Overton canvassed several ward organizations and civic clubs but found few who were willing to support him.[57] Without endorsements from Memphis's neighborhoods, Overton announced his retirement in August.[58] Up to this point he had been restrained in his public statements, but Overton could not resist a parting jab at Crump: "[H]e has convinced himself that he alone is responsible for the sunshine, good crops, and the gentle rains which fall from the heavens—no one may challenge his omnipotence.... I will never bow my knee to any tyrant. I will never raise my hand in the Nazi salute to any dictator."[59]

Crump anticipated a hard-fought contest and was thus surprised at Overton's decision. His first choice to represent the organization was fire and police commissioner Clifford Davis, but there was concern his former ties to the Ku Klux Klan would make a victory more difficult. Business leaders also feared Davis was not a strong enough leader to shoulder the burdens of higher office.[60] Shortly before Overton's withdrawal, Crump visited Walter Chandler at his home, where he asked the congressman if he would be willing to run for mayor. Chandler was reluctant to accept, but he told the Shelby leader, "Mr. Crump, I would not be where I am if it were not for you, and I am at your service."[61] Crump then left for a vacation in Battle Creek, Michigan, where he mulled over the final decision. While away he concluded Chandler was a better candidate than Davis.[62]

Chandler's candidacy was announced after Crump returned from his vacation. The pronouncement was made one day after President Roosevelt called a special session of Congress to repeal the Neutrality Act of 1935, which prevented the sale of arms to nations officially at war. The president wanted to help Great Britain and France in their war against Nazi Germany while avoiding American military involvement.[63] Roosevelt's proposal caused something of a problem for Crump. In order for Chandler to run for mayor, he was required by state law to resign his congressional seat. Crump did not want to hinder the president's motion, so he developed a novel approach to overcome this impediment. To the surprise of many, Crump announced he would run for mayor with the understanding that he would resign after his inauguration. Afterwards, the city commission would appoint Chandler to serve out Crump's term. Comparing this to a presidential contest, Crump stated, "I am simply an elector for Walter Chandler."[64] Political observers in Memphis, and throughout the nation, were amazed at Crump's announcement. Mississippi senator Pat Harrison wrote that his candidacy combined "political guts, a tincture of conspiracy against your enemies, a flavor of real patriotism, and much gratitude for a devoted friend. My congratulations go out to you."[65]

Apparently the remnants of the anti-Crump coalition were just as impressed, for no one rose to challenge his candidacy. Nevertheless, Crump wanted a large turnout for what became a referendum on his leadership. In order to garner voter enthusiasm, Crump and Hale organized a free celebration for the white citizens of Memphis. Similar to the event held in 1930 to celebrate Crump's congressional bid, the party drew thirty thousand Memphians to the fairgrounds.[66] Thirty-six thousand bottles of Coca-Cola, sixteen hundred gallons of lemonade, and all amusement rides were available for free to anyone who attended. In addition to the amusement rides, attendees witnessed fireworks, wrestling matches, and musical performances.[67] City employees worked the concessions, while two hundred volunteers from the Council of Civic Clubs provided crowd control.[68]

The large numbers of voters attending the celebration gave Crump cause for optimism as election day approached. The temperature reached an unseasonable seventy-six degrees as voters went to the polls. Ward captains expected a light turnout, but the voters of Memphis showed up in droves to cast ballots for Crump. The turnout was one of the highest in Memphis history, with Crump receiving 31,825 votes.[69] The overwhelming victory reinforced not only Crump's position in Memphis, but also his status as one of the most influential leaders in the United States. Meanwhile, the bizarre nature of the campaign continued as Memphis prepared to inaugurate its new mayor.

In addition to politics, the game of football was a great passion with Crump. He loved to attend local high school games with his family, and in late 1939 he planned to attend the Sugar Bowl in New Orleans. The game was scheduled for New Year's Day 1940, which was also the day of Memphis's mayoral inauguration. In order to accommodate Crump's schedule, the inauguration was held at midnight in a downtown train station. A light snow covered the Panama Limited train as a large party of well-wishers crowded the observation platform to see the historic occasion. Members of the organization threw snowballs as Crump strode up the platform with his daughter-in-law on his arm. Tom Crenshaw, deputy county court clerk, began to administer the oath but was interrupted when the mayor-elect called for his "old friend" Walter Chandler to join him. After taking the oath, Crump stated, "I wish to hand my resignation in and the city commission will elect an honorable, upright man that has real intelligence, Walter Chandler."[70]

Before he entered the train bound for New Orleans, Crump accepted a chrysanthemum from the Nineteenth Ward Crump Club. The boisterous crowd listened as he delivered a brief speech castigating newspapers for their alleged ties to communism. Crump then withdrew an invitation issued to the Congress of Industrial Organization's American Newspaper Guild to meet in Memphis. The crowd roared its approval as snowballs continued to fly. Crump shouted, "Goodbye, everyone" and entered the Panama Limited as someone in the crowd yelled, "God bless you, boss."

As the locomotive pulled out of the station and drove into the Mississippi darkness, perhaps Crump reflected on how far he had come since that train ride to Memphis in 1894. He had dreamed of greatness when he left Holly Springs, Mississippi, at the age of nineteen, and in many ways had achieved it. Through the exercise of great political acumen he played an important role in molding the city of Memphis into a modern southern metropolis. More importantly, in creating a biracial, multiethnic coalition within the segregated South, Crump influenced the evolution of American politics and can rightly be placed among the founders of the modern Democratic Party.

Afterword

"The Most Absolute Political Boss"

When Crump returned from New Orleans in early January 1940 his political organization was one of the most powerful in the United States. However, the circumstances that created the Crump machine soon began to change. The most noticeable difference was the lack of effective leadership below Crump. Up to the late 1930s Crump had relied heavily on the skill of the generalissimos. Overton, Rice, Hale, and McLain were often consulted and their views were weighed before a decision was made. Those who took their place, Mayor Chandler, public safety commissioner Joseph Boyle, and city attorney Will Gerber, were more likely to offer praise than useful advice. Even further, this new crop of organization leaders were afraid to do much without Crump's direct input. Writing in 1940, Chandler obsequiously sought Crump's approval: "Dear Mr. Crump: The City Commission has several matters on which we would like to have your judgment, and will appreciate an opportunity to see you on Monday, if convenient to you. I tried several times to reach you on the telephone today but your line was busy when I called."[1] Chandler's letter is indicative of the altered command structure of the organization. Crump expected fawning deference from his lieutenants and he chose men willing to give it.

The lack of skillful leadership combined with Crump's arrogance led to several disastrous decisions that obscured his earlier commitment to black voting rights. As discussed earlier, African American voters had offered their support in exchange for segregated access to city government and services. The nominal independence of black voters had not been an issue for the Shelby County organization until the 1938 Democratic primary. When several thousand African American voters cast ballots for Gordon Browning, the decision was made to outflank the independent-minded black leadership and replace them with those loyal to the organization. The first stage in this offensive was to sever ties with Robert Church, Jr. In 1939 the city seized Church's property holdings for back taxes, forcing the Republican leader to flee Memphis.[2] When Church's lieutenant, Dr. J. B. Martin, refused to curtail Church's political activities, he found his livelihood threatened as well.[3]

Commissioner Joseph Boyle ordered police officers to frisk every customer who entered Martin's drugstore on the pretense that illegal narcotics were sold there. Faced with the threat of arrest, Martin relocated to Chicago in 1940.[4] That same year, the Colored Democratic Club was formed under the chairmanship of Dr. J. E. Walker, who reported their political activities directly to E. W. Hale.[5] The combination of intimidation and coordination temporarily checked the desires of many African Americans who wished to free themselves of Crump's hegemony. However, their anger intensified when organization leaders prevented the president of the Brotherhood of Sleeping Car Porters, A. Philip Randolph, from speaking in Memphis in 1943.[6] Randolph returned the following spring, when he complained that Crump had "out-hitlered Hitler" in preventing him from speaking the previous year.[7] In an open letter challenging the Memphis leader to a debate on race relations, Randolph declared that Crump was "a symbol of Southern fascism that is a menace and danger to American democracy and hence must be exterminated."[8]

In 1947, the American Heritage Foundation sponsored a train, dubbed the "Freedom Train," which carried originals of the Declaration of Independence, the Constitution, and other historical documents across the nation to promote national unity and citizenship. The American Heritage Foundation forbade segregation and required that the locomotive be open to all citizens. Mayor James Pleasants, who had replaced Walter Chandler in 1946, canceled a stop in Memphis rather than allow integrated crowds access to their documentary heritage.[9] Many African Americans were outraged by this decision. Echoing A. Philip Randolph, the African Methodist Episcopal Ministers' Council charged that Mayor Pleasants sounded "more like Hitler than an American" when he announced the cancellation of the train's visit.[10] One year after the Freedom Train embarrassment, Crump experienced his worst political defeat since the 1919 city manager debacle.

In February 1948, Roosevelt's successor, Harry Truman, proposed several civil rights laws in a message to Congress. Included in the package was an antilynching proposal, abolition of the poll tax, a permanent fair employment practices committee, and the ending of segregation in interstate transportation. The president followed this message with an executive order in July ending racial separation in all federal agencies. Predictably, southern leaders howled in protest.[11] Crump was in that number and he joined with other key Democrats to try to deny Truman the party's presidential nomination. When that failed they formed the States' Rights Party, whose members the press dubbed "Dixiecrats." Crump campaigned vigorously on behalf of the States' Rights nominee, South Carolina governor J. Strom Thurmond,[12] but it had no appreciable impact. Thurmond was miserably defeated when Truman was reelected in the fall.

Meanwhile, Crump's political activities on the state level fared no better. In the 1948 Democratic primary, African Americans joined forces with an outraged white middle class to elect Gordon Browning governor. In many ways this was his greatest defeat, and it came about because he ignored the great lesson he had learned so well in 1927. Namely, to win elections in Shelby County one needed the support of the African American community and the white middle class. Between his inflated ego and bitter treatment of African Americans, Crump had developed a perfect recipe for electoral disaster. Crump remained a political force to be reckoned with until his death in 1954; nevertheless, after 1948 he was but a shell of the remarkable politician he had been in the 1930s.

The cumulative effect of these latest incidents severely tarnished his legacy. The national media gleefully painted Crump in the most unflattering terms, and historians blithely repeated their observations. For example, the *Chicago Tribune* exclaimed in a bold headline: *There Is a Fuehrer in Memphis*[13] and a writer for the *Economist* reported in 1943: "An entire generation has grown up in Memphis, and is now fighting on all battle fronts of the world, which has never taken part in any of the processes of democracy...."[14] In 1946 *Time* placed Crump on its cover, where he was described as "the most absolute political boss in the U.S."[15] Meanwhile, the African American press used his name as a byword for southern racism.[16]

Despite the vitriol of the national press, Crump was far more than an intemperate political boss. With his emphasis on municipal reform, Crump had much in common with other twentieth-century American mayors. Like Detroit's Hazen Pingree, Tom L. Johnson of Cleveland, and Toledo's Samuel "Golden Rule" Jones, Crump was committed to the public ownership of utilities and efficient government.[17] Although Crump was not the first American mayor to significantly emphasize social reform—Hazen Pingree of Detroit deserves that distinction[18]—Crump was arguably one of America's most

successful twentieth-century reform mayors. Through the skillful application of coalition politics, several progressive measures were
achieved for the Mississippi Delta's largest city, including a munici-
pally owned electric utility, flood control, public health improvements, and honest and efficient government.

In order to accomplish these goals, Crump did at times resort to
the type of unsavory tactics practiced by many urban political bosses
across the United States. The first half of the twentieth century constituted a kind of golden age of the urban Democratic Party boss,
with powerful political organizations emerging in Boston, Chicago,
Kansas City, Missouri, and Jersey City, New Jersey. Like his contem-
poraries James Michael Curley, Anton Cermak, Tom Pendergast,
and Frank Hague, Crump developed a broad-based coalition which
expanded the Democratic Party electorate and paved the way for
Franklin Roosevelt's New Deal.[19] Although they were similar in many
ways, there was one major difference between the leader of Memphis
and the bosses of Boston, Kansas City, and Jersey City. Crump's
organization remained assiduously honest, and, consequently, inefficiency and corruption failed to take root in the Bluff City.

Perhaps the political boss with whom Crump had the most in
common was Anton J. Cermak, who served as mayor of Chicago
from 1931 to 1933. During the 1920s Cermak built a multiethnic
Democratic Party organization which controlled the political fortunes of Cook County, Illinois. Reaching out to Eastern European
immigrants, Cermak recast the Illinois Democratic Party much as
Crump did in Tennessee with African Americans.[20] The two were
also similar in their unwavering commitment to reform. Like the
Memphis leader, Cermak eliminated government inefficiency and
brought needed public improvements to Chicago.[21] The major difference between these two remarkable men was that Cermak's Cook
County Democratic apparatus continued for several decades after

his death in 1933, while Crump's political organization did not survive his passing.

The impact of political collaboration between white and black voters in Shelby County was felt far beyond the borders of Tennessee. Although it was a strictly segregated society, the color line was drawn differently in Memphis. Crump's ambition, combined with the tenacity of Memphis blacks, in effect pushed back the color line to allow African Americans participation in the political process. Black voters in Memphis took full advantage of this situation and carved out a small measure of citizenship within a racist social structure. Owing to his great political skill, Crump convinced a large number of these blacks to abandon their allegiance to the Republicans for the party of Franklin D. Roosevelt. Close attention to political conditions in Shelby County was paid by James Farley and other Democratic strategists who followed Crump's example when refashioning the national Democratic Party in 1936. Although not the architect, Edward Hull Crump was one of the most important builders of the modern Democratic Party and thus was an important element in the transformation of American democracy in the 1930s.

Appendix

Election Returns—Memphis Mayor—1909–1939

1909
5,894—E. H. Crump
5,815—J. J. Williams

1911
11,432—E. H. Crump
3,536—J. J. Williams

1915
3,572—E. H. Crump
522—W. A. Weatherall

1918
3,665—Frank L. Monteverde
1,576—George A. Macon

1919
11,052—Rowlett Paine
8,350—J. J. Williams

1923
12,409—Rowlett Paine
7,816—W. Joe Wood
2,947—L. T. Fitzhugh

1927

19,548—Watkins Overton

6,948—Rowlett Paine

1931

23,684—Watkins Overton

869—C. C. Pashby

1935

11,086—Watkins Overton

No opponent

1939

31,825—E. H. Crump

No opponent

Source: *Memphis Commercial Appeal*

Election Returns—Shelby County Trustee—1916–1922

1916

8,170—E. H. Crump

6,550—Harry Litty

1918

5,008—E. H. Crump

2,718—W. C. Edmondson

1920

12,515—E. H. Crump

4,532—Martin Boyd

1922

9,548—E. H. Crump

3,408—Martin Boyd

Source: *Memphis Commercial Appeal*

Election Returns—Shelby County Democratic Primary—1920–1938

1920

Tennessee Governor

8,840—Austin Peay

5,800—L. E. Gwinn

1,723—Benton McMillin

U. S. Senate (Short Term)

11,619—Kenneth D. McKellar

3,611—G. T. Fitzhugh

1922

Tennessee Governor

9,405—Austin Peay

3,243—L. E. Gwinn

1,838—Benton McMillin

U. S. Senate

12,399—Kenneth D. McKellar

3,729—G. T. Fitzhugh

1924

Tennessee Governor

14,391—Austin Peay

1926

Tennessee Governor

15,748—Hill McAlister

3,677—Austin Peay

1928

Tennessee Governor

23,600—Hill McAlister

3,550—Henry Horton

240—Lewis Pope

U. S. Senate
24,292—Kenneth D. McKellar
2,379—Finis J. Garrett

1930
Tennessee Governor
27,475—Henry Horton
2,245—L. E. Gwinn

1932
Tennessee Governor
25,772—Hill McAlister
7,534—Malcolm Patterson
2,179—Lewis Pope

U. S. House of Representatives
28,522—E. H. Crump
5,695—Thomas Collier

1934
Tennessee Governor
39,646—Hill McAlister
3,432—Lewis Pope

U. S. Senate (Long Term)
40,775—Kenneth D. McKellar
1,274—John R. Neal

U. S. Senate (Short Term)
38,150—Nathan Bachman
4,376—Gordon Browning

U. S. House of Representatives
39,387—Walter Chandler
1,633—Thomas Collier
370—S. A. Godsey

1936
Tennessee Governor
60,218—Gordon Browning
861—Burgin Dossett
39—C. W. Wright

U. S. Senate
59,669—Nathan Bachman
694—John R. Neal

1938
Tennessee Governor
56,302—Prentice Cooper
9,214—Gordon Browning

Notes

Foreword

1. William D. Miller, *Mr. Crump of Memphis* (Baton Rouge: Louisiana State University Press, 1964), 3–26, 31.
2. Mollie Nelms Crump to E. H. Crump, n. d., E. H. Crump Collection, Memphis Public Library and Information Center.
3. Ibid.
4. Beverly G. Bond and Janann Sherman, *Memphis in Black and White* (Charleston: Arcadia, 2003), 26, 33–34.
5. Robert A. Sigafoos, *Cotton Row to Beale Street* (Memphis: Memphis State University Press, 1979), 44–45.
6. Gerald M. Capers, Jr., *The Biography of a River Town: Memphis, Its Heroic Age* (New Orleans: Tulane University Press, 1966), 177–78; Bond and Sherman, *Memphis in Black and White*, 59–60.
7. *New York Sunday Mercury*, 10 October 1870, reprinted in the *Memphis Commercial Appeal*, 10 October 1970.
8. Bond and Sherman, *Memphis in Black and White*, 66–70.
9. Miller, *Mr. Crump of Memphis*, 37–42.
10. Ibid., 54–56.
11. William D. Miller, *Memphis During the Progressive Era* (Memphis: Memphis State University Press, 1957), 138–39.
12. Miller, *Mr. Crump of Memphis*, 56–57.

"A Business Government by a Business Man"

1. Miller, *Mr. Crump of Memphis*, 58–59.
2. Ibid.

119

3. Ibid.

4. Wayne Dowdy, "E. H. Crump and the Mayors of Memphis," *West Tennessee Historical Society Papers* 53 (1999), 80.

5. Bradley Robert Rice, *Progressive Cities: The Commission Government Movement in America, 1901–1920* (Austin: University of Texas Press, 1977), xiii–xiv.

6. Miller, *Mr. Crump of Memphis*, 58–59.

7. Ibid., 73.

8. *Memphis News-Scimitar*, 26 September 1909.

9. Miller, *Memphis during the Progressive Era*, 132–37, 144–45.

10. *Memphis Commercial Appeal*, 1 November 1909.

11. Ibid., 4 November 1909.

12. Miller, *Mr. Crump of Memphis*, 74.

13. *Memphis Commercial Appeal*, 5 November 1909.

14. Ibid., 9 November 1909; Miller, *Mr. Crump of Memphis*, 74.

15. Petition of J. J. Williams contesting election of Hon. E. H. Crump as mayor, 13 November 1909, Loose Papers of the Memphis Legislative Council, Shelby County Archives.

16. Ibid.

17. Resolution Fixing Date for Hearing of Williams Versus Crump, n.d.; and Motion of Edward H. Crump to dismiss the petition, 22 November 1909, Loose Papers of the Memphis Legislative Council; *Memphis Commercial Appeal*, 23 November 1909.

18. *Memphis Commercial Appeal*, 2 January 1910.

19. Meeting Minutes of the Memphis Board of Commissioners, 1 January 1910, Loose Papers of the Memphis Board of Commissioners, Shelby County Archives.

20. Rules and regulations governing examinations to be held by the civil service commissioners, 10 May 1910, Loose Papers of the Memphis Board of Commissioners.

21. Miller, *Mr. Crump of Memphis*, 79.

22. E. H. Crump to George King, 15 July 1915, Crump Collection.

23. Miller, *Mr. Crump of Memphis*, 80–81.

24. Mayor E. H. Crump to the Board of City Commissioners, 31 December 1912, Loose Papers of the Memphis Board of Commissioners.

25. Miller, *Memphis during the Progressive Era*, 167–168.

26. Mayor's Statement on Prohibition, 1914, Crump Collection.

27. J. A. Fowler to E. H. Crump, 4 May 1914, Crump Collection.

28. Anti-Saloon and Law Enforcement League Chairman J. W. McKinney to Mayor E. H. Crump, 2 May 1914, E. H. Crump Collection.

29. An Ordinance to Prescribe the Use of Proper Headlights on Street Railway Cars and Locomotive Engines, 17 February 1910, Loose Papers of the Memphis Board of Commissioners.

30. Miller, *Memphis during the Progressive Era*, 163.

31. Memphis Board of Commissioners, Minute Book A, 1 January 1910–2 March 1911, 46.

32. Memphis Board of Commissioners, Minute Book A, Interurban Ordinance, 4 October 1910, 470; Miller, *Mr. Crump of Memphis*, 93–94.

33. Miller, *Mr. Crump of Memphis*, 94–95.

34. An ordinance to provide the hours during which boot-black stands employing boys under the age of 18 years shall keep open in the City of Memphis, 18 July 1911, Loose Papers of the Memphis Board of Commissioners.

35. Richard W. Hepler, "Bovine Tuberculosis and the Battle for Pure Milk in Memphis, 1910–1911," *West Tennessee Historical Society Papers* 40 (1986), 6–23.

36. An Ordinance to Prevent the Spread of Infectious, Communicable, and Contagious Diseases among School Children, Loose Papers of the Memphis Board of Commissioners.

37. An Ordinance to Regulate the Practice of Mid-Wifery as a Profession, 9 August 1910, Loose Papers of the Memphis Board of Commissioners.

38. Memphis Board of Commissioners, *One Year and Eight Months under Commission Government* (Memphis, 1911).

39. E. H. Crump to Dan C. Newton, 5 May 1910, Loose Papers of the Memphis Board of Commissioners.

40. An Ordinance to Provide for a Board of Charities for the City of Memphis, 27 December 1910, Loose Papers of the Memphis Board of Commissioners.

41. *One Year and Eight Months under Commission Government.*

42. Ibid.

43. Lamar Whitlow Bridges, "Editor Mooney Versus Boss Crump," *West Tennessee Historical Society Papers* 20 (1966), 77–107.

44. Ibid.

45. *Memphis Commercial Appeal*, 27 October 1911.

46. T. J. Searcy to E. H. Crump, 8 July 1915, Crump Collection.

47. E. H. Crump to T. J. Searcy, 9 July 1915, Crump Collection.

48. Allen H. Kitchens, "Ouster of Mayor Edward H. Crump, 1915–1916," *West Tennessee Historical Society Papers* 19 (1965), 105–20.

49. Lester C. Lamon, *Black Tennesseans, 1900–1930* (Knoxville: University of Tennessee Press, 1977), 222–23; Harry H. Pace to E. H. Crump, 6 July 1911, Crump Collection.

50. Resolution Relative to the Purchase of a Park for Negroes, 13 June 1911, Loose Papers of the Memphis Board of Commissioners.

51. *Memphis Commercial Appeal*, 8 November 1911; Bridges, "Editor Mooney versus Boss Crump," 77–107.

52. Robert E. Moran to E. H. Crump, 27 October 1911, R. F. LaCroix to E. H. Crump, 31 October 1911, L. A. Montedonico to E. H. Crump, 6 November 1911, Crump Collection.

53. B. C. Hinds to E. H. Crump, 7 November 1911, Crump Collection.

54. J. M. Fly to the managers of Mr. Bowers' Stores, 4 November 1911, Crump Collection.

55. Lamar Park Improvement Club Vice President W. H. Buck to E. H. Crump, 9 April 1914, Crump Collection.

56. *City Club Bulletin*, January 22, 1927.

57. E. H. Crump to City Club Secretary Thomas B. Blake, 29 November 1913 and Thomas B. Blake to E. H. Crump, 4 December 1913, Crump Collection.

58. Timothy P. Ezell, "Patterson, Malcolm R." in Carroll Van West, ed., *The Tennessee Encyclopedia of History and Culture* (Nashville: Tennessee Historical Society, 1998), 725.

59. Phillip Langsdon, *Tennessee: A Political History* (Franklin: Hillboro Press, 2000), 263–65.

60. E. H. Crump to Luke Lea, 28 May 1912, Crump Collection; Langsdon, *Tennessee: A Political History*, 271.

61. E. H. Crump to J. M. Goodbar, 22 June 1912, Crump Collection.

62. E. H. Crump to T. R. Preston, 4 July 1912, Crump Collection.

63. *Memphis Commercial Appeal*, 2 August 1912.

64. E. H. Crump to W. J. Bass, 23 October 1912, Crump Collection.

65. Ibid., 4 November 1912, Crump Collection.

66. *Memphis Commercial Appeal*, 7 November 1912.

67. Ibid.

68. R. O. Johnston to E. H. Crump, 31 January 1912, Crump Collection.

69. Frank Dibrell, *Dibrell Vs. Crump* (Nashville: 1912), housed in the E. H. Crump Collection.

70. Ibid., 7.

71. Ibid., 2.

72. E. H. Crump to Frank Dibrell, 13 February 1912.

73. C. D. Mitchell to E. H. Crump, 30 January 1912, Henry H. Horton to E. H. Crump, 10 March 1912, Crump Collection.

74. Frank Dibrell to E. H. Crump, 20 February 1912, Crump Collection.

75. *Memphis Commercial Appeal*, 7 January 1913.

76. Langsdon, *Tennessee: A Political History*, 281.

77. *Memphis Commercial Appeal*, 14 January 1913, M. F. Dobbins to E. H. Crump, 14 January 1913, Crump Collection.

78. E. H. Crump to Kenneth McKellar, 12 April 1912, Kenneth McKellar Collection, Memphis Public Library and Information Center.

79. E. H. Crump to Kenneth McKellar, 8 April 1912, McKellar Collection.

80. E. H. Crump to Owen Lilly et al., 27 April 1912, Crump Collection; *Memphis Commercial Appeal*, 3 April 1912.

81. *Memphis Commercial Appeal*, 2 April 1912.

82. Luke Lea to E. H. Crump, 6 April 1912, Crump Collection.

83. E. H. Crump to Kenneth McKellar, 25 June 1912, and 14 December 1914, McKellar Collection.

84. An Ordinance to Regulate the Charges for Telephone Service in the City of Memphis, 5 March 1912, Loose Papers of the Memphis Board of Commissioners.

85. E. H. Crump to W. B. Marr, 1 November 1913, Crump Collection.

86. An Ordinance to Regulate the Charges to be made by Public Vehicles Carrying Passengers for Hire, 31 December 1912, Loose Papers of the Memphis Board of Commissioners.

87. An Ordinance to Further Regulate and Control the operation of Street Railway cars for the Safety of the General Public, 13 January 1914, Loose Papers of the Memphis Board of Commissioners.

88. An Ordinance to Regulate and Control the Operation of Street Railway Cars so as to provide for Greater Comfort and Safety of Passengers, 13 January 1914, Loose Papers of the Memphis Board of Commissioners.

89. An Ordinance to require the Owners and Occupants of Property to Keep the Sidewalks Clean in Front of the Premises Owned or Occupied, 24 March 1914, Loose Papers of the Memphis Board of Commissioners.

90. An Ordinance to Amend an Ordinance entitled "an Ordinance to Regulate the installation of Electric Wiring in Certain Buildings in the City of Memphis and to Provide for the Violation of this Ordinance" by Changing the Limits and Classes of Buildings Affected, 7 April 1914, Loose Papers of the Memphis Board of Commissioners.

91. Walter Goodman to E. H. Crump, 18 December 1912, Loose Papers of the Memphis Board of Commissioners.

92. An Ordinance to Regulate the furnishing of water free or at reduced rates, 29 September 1914, Loose Papers of the Memphis Board of Commissioners.

93. Petition of the Colored Men's Civic League, 8 April 1914, Crump Collection.

94. *Memphis News Scimitar*, 9 April 1914.

95. Kitchens, "Ouster of Mayor Edward H. Crump," 106.

96. Ibid., 107.

97. Miller, *Memphis during the Progressive Era*, 165.

98. Kitchens, "Ouster of Mayor Edward H. Crump," 108.

99. Ibid., 106.

100. Z. N. Estes to E. H. Crump, 30 October 1911, Crump Collection.

101. Ibid.

102. E. H. Crump to the Democratic Executive Committee of Shelby County, 10 July 1914, Crump Collection.

103. *Memphis Commercial Appeal*, 11 July 1914.

104. Bridges, "Editor Mooney versus Boss Crump," 77–107.

105. Charles M. Bryan to E. H. Crump, 27 July 1914, Crump Collection.

106. Miller, *Mr. Crump of Memphis*, 106.

107. Langsdon, *Tennessee: A Political History*, 287.

108. E. H. Crump to W. T. Kennerly, 22 August 1912, Crump Collection.

109. Langsdon, *Tennessee: A Political History*, 289.

110. Porter Dunlap to E. H. Crump, 5 November 1914; L. D. Hill to E. H. Crump, 11 November 1914, Crump Collection.

111. Z. N. Estes to editor of the *Camden Citizen*, 1 January 1915; E. H. Crump to Eugene Travis, 20 January 1915, Crump Collection.

112. T. C. Ashcroft to E. H. Crump with attached Elkins Ouster Bill, 15 January 1915, Crump Collection; Kitchens, "Ouster of Mayor Edward H. Crump," 105–120.

113. T. C. Ashcroft to E. H. Crump, 3 February 1915, Crump Collection.

114. Marvin Pope to E. H. Crump, 19 August 1915, Crump Collection.

115. Ibid.

116. Surveillance Report on the Activities of the Honorable Frank Thompson, n.d., Crump Collection.

117. Kitchens, "Ouster of Mayor Edward H. Crump," 105–120.

118. E. H. Crump to W. H. Cummings, 10 November 1915, Crump Collection.

119. Kitchens, "Ouster of Mayor Edward H. Crump," 105–120.

120. Ibid.

121. Ibid.

"The Black Flag of Machine Politics"

1. James H. Patton to E. H. Crump, 8 September 1915; E. H. Crump to James H. Patton, 9 September 1915, Crump Collection.

2. *Memphis Commercial Appeal*, 23 July 1916.

3. Ibid., 11 July 1916.

4. Ibid., 23 July 1916.

5. Ibid., 25 July 1916.

6. Ibid., 26 July 1916.

7. Ibid., 27 July 1916.

8. Ibid., 15 July 1916.

9. Ibid., 3 August 1916.

10. Ibid.

11. Ibid.

12. Ibid.

13. Joe Walk, *Memphis Executive and Legislative Government* (Memphis: 1996), 65–66.

14. Dowdy, "E. H. Crump and the Mayors of Memphis," 83.

15. Ibid.

16. Walk, *Memphis Executive and Legislative Government*, 65–66.

17. *Memphis Commercial Appeal*, 6 April 1918.

18. Ibid., 1 August 1918.

19. Ibid.

20. *Memphis Commercial Appeal*, 2 August 1918.

21. Summary of the Minutes of the July 6, 1918, meeting of the Shelby County Democratic Executive Committee, 13 January 1919, Crump Collection.

22. Citizen's Committee of One Hundred, *Proposed Bill Providing the Council-Manager Plan of Government for the City of Memphis* (Memphis, 1919) housed in the Crump Collection; "City Manager Drive is Recalled by Paine," *Memphis Commercial Appeal*, 27 April 1949.

23. *Memphis Commercial Appeal*, 20 March 1919.

24. Hill McAlister to E. H. Crump, 13 March 1919, Crump Collection.

25. Carl Larsen to E. H. Crump, 9 March 1919, Crump Collection.

26. E. H. Crump to appeals court judge W. W. Faw, 1 March 1919, Crump Collection.

27. *Memphis Commercial Appeal*, 25 March 1919.

28. Ibid.

29. *Memphis Commercial Appeal*, 10 April 1919.

30. Ibid.

31. *Memphis Commercial Appeal*, 15 August 1919.

32. Citizens Ticket Brochure, "Will You Vote for Williams and High Taxes?," 1919, Crump Collection.

33. Dowdy, "E. H. Crump and the Mayors of Memphis," 84.

34. Carol Lynn Yellin and Janann Sherman, *The Perfect 36: Tennessee Delivers Woman Suffrage* (Memphis: Serviceberry Press, 1998), 129, 131; E. H. Crump to Mrs. John M. Kenny, 2 August 1920, Crump Collection; Kenneth McKellar to E. H. Crump, 20 December 1920, McKellar Collection.

35. Dewey W. Grantham, "Tennessee and Twentieth-Century American Politics," in Carroll Van West, *Tennessee History: The Land, the People, and the Culture* (Knoxville: University of Tennessee Press, 1998), 349.

36. *Memphis News-Scimitar*, 31 May 1922.

37. *Memphis Commercial Appeal*, 5 August 1922.

38. *Memphis News-Scimitar*, 17 June and 20 June 1922.

39. Ibid., 26 June 1922.

40. Ibid., 27 June 1922.

41. Ibid., 3 July 1922.

42. Ibid., 13 July 1922.

43. *Memphis Commercial Appeal*, 5 August 1922.

44. Ibid.

45. *Memphis News-Scimitar*, 30 October 1922.

46. Ibid.

47. *Memphis News-Scimitar*, 2 November 1922.

48. *Memphis Commercial Appeal*, 6 November 1922.

49. Ibid.

50. *Memphis Commercial Appeal*, 7 November 1922; David D. Lee, *Tennessee in Turmoil: Politics in the Volunteer State, 1920–1932* (Memphis: Memphis State University Press, 1979), 34.

51. *Memphis Commercial Appeal*, 8 November 1922.

52. Ibid., 7 November 1922.

53. Ibid., 8 November 1922; *Memphis News-Scimitar*, 8 November 1922.

54. *Memphis Commercial Appeal*, 24 March 1923.

55. Ibid.

56. *Memphis Commercial Appeal*, 27 March 1923.

57. Ibid.

58. Lee, *Tennessee in Turmoil*, 43.

59. *Memphis Commercial Appeal*, 25 March 1923.

60. Lee, *Tennessee in Turmoil*, 44.

61. Ibid.; *Memphis Commercial Appeal*, 1 April 1923.

62. Lee, *Tennessee in Turmoil*, 44.

63. Virginia Phillips, "Rowlett Paine, Mayor of Memphis, 1920–1924," *West Tennessee Historical Society Papers* 13 (1959), 95–116.

64. Memorandum of Rowlett Paine's Mayoral Failures, n. d., Crump Collection.

65. *Memphis News-Scimitar*, 23 September 1923.

66. Ibid., 5 October 1923.

67. Ibid., 6 October 1923.

68. Kenneth T. Jackson, *The Ku Klux Klan in the City, 1915–1930* (New York: Oxford University Press, 1967), 46–48; copy of Memphis Klan # 3 Ballot, 11 September 1923, Crump Collection.

69. Jackson, *Ku Klux Klan in the City*, 50.

70. Statement of Clifford Davis, 1923, Crump Collection; *Memphis News-Scimitar*, 1 October 1923.

71. *Memphis News-Scimitar*, 6 October 1923.

72. Jackson, *Ku Klux Klan in the City*, 50–51.

73. Ibid., 46–47.

74. Lester C. Lamon, *Black Tennesseans, 1900–1930* (Knoxville: University of Tennessee Press, 1977), 44.

75. *Memphis Commercial Appeal*, 2 November 1923.

76. Ibid., 6 November 1923.

77. Ibid., 29 October 1923.

78. Ibid., 1 November 1923.

79. Ibid., 7 November 1923.

80. Ibid., 9 November 1923; Lamon, *Black Tennesseans, 1900–1930*, 44.

"The People Have Made Their Statement"

1. Woodrow Wilson to E. H. Crump, 3 January 1916, Crump Collection.

2. Tom Bagley to Kenneth McKellar, 18 March 1924, McKellar Collection.

3. William S. Shields to E. H. Crump, 10 March 1924, McKellar Collection.

4. E. H. Crump to Kenneth McKellar, 19 March 1924, McKellar Collection.

5. Ibid., 11 March 1924, McKellar Collection.

6. Joe V. Williams to E. H. Crump, 3 June 1924, Crump Collection.

7. Ibid.

8. William G. McAdoo to E. H. Crump, 12 June 1924, Crump Collection.

9. T. K. Riddick to E. H. Crump, 27 June 1924; E. H. Crump to Kenneth McKellar, 9 September 1924, Crump Collection.

10. E. H. Crump to secretary for Governor Franklin D. Roosevelt, 27 October 1931, Crump Collection.

11. Miller, *Mr. Crump of Memphis*, 138–39.

12. E. H. Crump to David I. Walsh, 6 November 1924, Crump Collection.

13. Kenneth McKellar to E. H. Crump, 8 February 1924, McKellar Collection.

14. Lee, *Tennessee in Turmoil*, 46.

15. *Memphis Commercial Appeal*, 8 August 1924.

16. E. H. Crump to Kenneth McKellar, 8 January 1924, McKellar Collection; *Memphis Commercial Appeal*, 8 January 1924.

17. E. H. Crump to J. T. Williams, 4 August 1924; E. H. Crump to J. Frank White, 4 August 1924; E. H. Crump to W. F. Russell, 5 August 1924, Crump Collection.

18. *Memphis Commercial Appeal*, 6 August 1924.

19. Jackson, *Ku Klux Klan in the City*, 57; *Memphis Commercial Appeal*, 8 August 1924.

20. E. H. Crump to Mrs. J. A. Riechman, 19 August 1924, Crump Collection.

21. J. D. Hunt to E. H. Crump, 9 May 1925; E. H. Crump to Jeff D. Hunt, 13 May 1925, Crump Collection.

22. Hilary Howse to E. H. Crump, 24 June 1925, Crump Collection.

23. *Memphis Commercial Appeal*, 18 July 1926.

24. Ibid., 5 August 1926.

25. Ibid., 18 July 1926.

26. Ibid., 23 July and 1 August 1926.

27. Ibid., 5 August 1926.

28. Lee, *Tennessee in Turmoil*, 74–76.

29. *Memphis Commercial Appeal*, 28 June 1927; *Memphis Evening Appeal*, 28 June 1927.

30. *Memphis Evening Appeal*, 28 June 1927.

31. Ibid.

32. *Memphis Evening Appeal*, 2 July 1927.

33. John B. Vesey to E. H. Crump, 31 October 1927, Crump Collection; *Memphis Evening Appeal*, 5 July 1927.

34. *Memphis Commercial Appeal*, 3 July 1927.

35. *Memphis Evening Appeal*, 7 July 1927.

36. Ibid., 11 July 1927.

37. Ibid.

38. *Memphis Evening Appeal*, 25 July 1927.

39. E. H. Crump to Kenneth McKellar, 28 January 1927, McKellar Collection.

40. *Memphis Evening Appeal*, 30 July 1927.

41. Ibid.

42. Ibid.

43. E. H. Crump to Betty Crump, 5 August 1927, Crump Collection.

44. *Memphis Evening Appeal*, 16 August 1927.

45. Ibid.

46. *Memphis Evening Appeal*, 28 June 1927.

47. Ibid., 16 August 1927.

48. Ibid., 20 August 1927.

49. E. H. Crump to Betty Crump, 27 August 1927, Crump Collection.

50. Friends of the Watkins Overton-Cliff Davis Ticket, "Are You Interested in Lower Taxes?," campaign circular housed in the Crump Collection.

51. *Memphis Evening Appeal*, 31 August 1927.

52. C. B. Blackwell to Edward W. Slater, 5 September 1927, Crump Collection.

53. E. H. Crump to Twenty-ninth Ward Overton-Davis Club president J. F Douthit, 14 September 1927, Crump Collection; and *Memphis Commercial Appeal*, 7 September 1927.

54. *Memphis Evening Appeal*, 21 October 1927; *Memphis Commercial Appeal*, 22 October 1927.

55. *Memphis Evening Appeal*, 19 August 1927.

56. David M. Tucker, *Lieutenant Lee of Beale Street* (Nashville: Vanderbilt University Press, 1971), 93.

57. Ibid.

58. *Memphis Commercial Appeal*, 9 September 1927.

59. George W. Lee 1967 interview, Everett R. Cook Oral History Collection, Memphis Public Library and Information Center.

60. *Memphis Commercial Appeal*, 9 September 1927.

61. Mrs. T. S. Brown to E. H. Crump, 1 September 1927, Crump Collection.

62. E. H. Crump to Mrs. T. S. Brown, 2 September 1927, Crump Collection.

63. Ibid.

64. *Memphis Evening Appeal*, 9 September 1927.

65. Ibid.

66. *Memphis Evening Appeal*, 1 November 1927.

67. Ibid., 5 October 1927.

68. Ibid., 22 September 1927.

69. Detective Sergeant E. M. Crumby to chief of police J. B. Burney, 21 September 1927, Crump Collection.

70. Ibid.

71. *Memphis Evening Appeal*, 24 September 1927.

72. Ibid.

73. *Memphis Evening Appeal*, 1 October 1927.

74. Ibid., 11 October 1927.

75. Ibid., 12 October 1927.

76. Ibid., 11 October 1927.

77. Ibid., 12 October 1927.

78. Ibid.

79. Ibid.

80. *Memphis Evening Appeal*, 15 October 1927.

81. Ibid., 17 October 1927.

82. Ibid., 19 November 1927.

83. Ibid., 20 October 1927.

84. Ibid., 3 November 1927.

85. Joseph M. Fly to E. H. Crump, 6 September 1927, Crump Collection.

86. E. H. Crump to Overton-Davis campaign chairman Walter Chandler, 5 October 1927, Crump Collection.

87. *Memphis Evening Appeal*, 1 October 1927.

88. Ibid., 31 October 1927.

89. *Memphis Commercial Appeal,* 11 November 1927.

90. E. H. Crump to Frank J. Rice, 17 October 1927, Crump Collection.

91. *Memphis Commercial Appeal,* 11 November 1927; *Memphis Evening Appeal,* 11 November 1927.

92. *Memphis Commercial Appeal,* 11 November 1927.

93. Ibid.; E. H. Crump to Sid A. Guy, 14 November 1927, Crump Collection.

"A Good Tammany Hall Tennessean"

1. Political advertisement, "Read Overton-Davis Platform—Progressive for a Big City," Walter Chandler Papers, Memphis Public Library and Information Center.

2. "An Ordinance to Create An Airport Commission for the City of Memphis," 3 April 1928, Memphis Board of Commissioners, Minute Book K: 233, Shelby County Archives.

3. Memphis Board of Commissioners, Minute Book K: 443.

4. Municipal Reference Library, *Municipal Progress in Memphis* (City of Memphis, 1937), 13.

5. Andrew A. Bruce and Thomas S. Fitzgerald, *A Study of Crime in the City of Memphis, Tennessee* (Chicago: Northwestern University Press, 1928), 3.

6. *Memphis Evening Appeal,* 19 May 1928.

7. Ibid., 4 May 1928.

8. Ibid.

9. *Memphis Evening Appeal,* 14 and 15 May 1928.

10. *Memphis Commercial Appeal,* 6 March 1928.

11. Ibid., 8 March 1928.

12. Ibid., 10 March 1928.

13. Ibid., 24 February 1929.

14. Selma S. Lewis, *A Biblical People in the Bible Belt: The Jewish Community of Memphis, Tennessee, 1840s–1960s* (Macon: Mercer University Press, 1998), 69.

15. E. H. Crump to J. H. Slaton, 14 May 1915, Crump Collection.

16. A. L. Lowenstein to E. H. Crump, 13 May 1915, Crump Collection.

17. *Memphis Commercial Appeal,* 25 June 1936.

18. Lloyd T. Binford to all Motion Picture Managers City of Memphis, 24 June 1936, Watkins Overton Papers, Memphis Public Library and Information Center.

19. Lester Velie, "You Can't See That Movie: Censorship in Action," *Collier's*, 6 May 1950.

20. *Memphis Commercial Appeal*, 10 December 1947.

21. For a more detailed look at Binford and movie censorship in Memphis, see G. Wayne Dowdy, "Censoring Popular Culture: Political and Social Control in Segregated Memphis," *West Tennessee Historical Society Papers* 55 (2001), 98–117.

22. E. H. Crump to the editor of the *Nashville Banner*, 24 August 1928, Crump Collection.

23. *Memphis Evening Appeal*, 3 August 1928.

24. Ibid., 4 August 1928.

25. Ibid.; Lee, *Tennessee in Turmoil*, 96.

26. *Memphis Evening Appeal*, 29 August 1928.

27. Ibid., 7 August 1928.

28. Louise Gambill, *Memphis in the Heart of the Mid-South: A Story of Progress Made Possible by Taxes* (Memphis: E. H. Clarke Company, 1935), 8.

29. Ibid.

30. Robert A. Sigafoos, *Cotton Row to Beale Street: A Business History of Memphis* (Memphis: Memphis State University Press, 1979), 167.

31. Roger Biles, *Memphis in the Great Depression* (Memphis: Memphis State University Press, 1986), 56–57.

32. Ibid., 57–58.

33. E. H. Crump to Kenneth McKellar, 3 June 1930, McKellar Collection.

34. Kenneth McKellar to E. H. Crump, 29 May 1930, McKellar Collection.

35. *Memphis Commercial Appeal*, 10 June 1930.

36. Ibid., 11 June 1930.

37. Lee, *Tennessee in Turmoil*, 106.

38. *Memphis Commercial Appeal*, 22 July 1930.

39. Memphis Council of Civic Clubs, *1935 Annual* (Memphis: 1935), 19–35.

40. Ibid., 12.

41. Ibid., 6,12.

42. Ibid., 12.

43. E. H. Crump to W. T. McLain, 13 April 1933, Crump Collection.

44. Gloria Brown Melton, "Blacks in Memphis, Tennessee 1920–1955" (Ph. D. dissertation, Washington State University, 1982), 100,174.

45. Petition "To the Honorable Mayor, City and Park Commissioners of the City of Memphis, Tennessee," 1930, Watkins Overton Papers, Memphis Public Library and Information Center.

46. "Bob Church in Doorway of Court Sees Reckless Driving Charges Dropped," *Memphis Commercial Appeal*, 9 July 1933.

47. George W. Lee 1967 Interview, Everett R. Cook Oral History Collection, Memphis Public Library and Information Center.

48. *Memphis Commercial Appeal*, 26 July 1930.

49. Ibid., 9 August 1930.

50. Ibid., 22 and 24 October 1930.

51. Ibid., 21 and 22 August 1930.

52. David Burner, *Herbert Hoover: A Public Life* (New York: Knopf, 1979), 193–95.

53. *Memphis Commercial Appeal*, 21 October 1930.

54. E. H. Crump to Kenneth McKellar, 3 December 1930, McKellar Collection.

55. *Memphis Commercial Appeal*, 23 and 24 October, 2 November 1930.

56. Ibid., 6 November 1930.

57. Lee, *Tennessee in Turmoil*, 115–16.

58. Ibid., 130–31.

59. E. H. Crump to Kenneth McKellar, 17 January 1931, McKellar Collection.

60. Lee, *Tennessee in Turmoil*, 118.

61. Ibid., 130–31.

62. *Memphis Commercial Appeal*, 14 May 1931.

63. E. H. Crump to Herbert Hoover, 24 June 1931, Crump Collection.

64. E. H. Crump to Roane Waring, 26 June 1931, Roane Waring Collection, Memphis Public Library and Information Center.

65. *Memphis Commercial Appeal*, 1 August 1931.

66. Ibid., 29 August 1931.

67. Ibid., 15 August 1931.

68. Ibid., 11 and 29 October 1931.

69. Ibid., 3 November 1931.

70. Ibid., 6 November 1931.

71. *Memphis Evening Appeal*, 8 April 1932.

72. Ibid., 13 April 1932.

73. E. H. Crump to Watkins Overton, 3 March 1933, Crump Collection; *Memphis Evening Appeal*, 2 December 1932; Ann B. Irish, *Joseph W. Byrns of Tennessee* (Knoxville: University of Tennessee Press, 2001), 152–53.

74. John Nance Garner to E. W. Hale, 1 April 1933, Crump Collection; Steve Neal, *Happy Days Are Here Again: The 1932 Democratic Convention, the Emergence of FDR and How America Was Changed Forever* (New York: William Morrow, 2004), 91–93.

75. E. H. Crump to Watkins Overton, 5 May 1932, Watkins Overton Collection, University of Memphis.

76. E. H. Crump to Watkins Overton, 17 March 1932; Ralph Picard to E. H. Crump, 5 May 1932, Overton Collection.

77. Lyle W. Dorsett, *Franklin D. Roosevelt and the City Bosses* (Port Washington: Kennikat Press, 1977), 35–36.

78. E. H. Crump to secretary to Governor Franklin D. Roosevelt, 27 October 1931, E. H. Crump Collection; Timothy S. Huebner, "Mr. Crump Goes to Washington," paper presented at the E. H. Crump Symposium, 23 October 2004.

79. Dorsett, *Franklin D. Roosevelt and the City Bosses*, 18.

80. Louis Howe to E. H. Crump, 1 December 1931, E. H. Crump Collection.

81. E. H. Crump to personal secretary to Governor Franklin D. Roosevelt, 13 January 1932, Crump Collection.

82. Clyde Shropshire to E. H. Crump, 1 March 1932, Crump Collection.

83. Franklin D. Roosevelt to E. H. Crump, 22 March 1932, Crump Collection.

84. E. H. Crump to Franklin D. Roosevelt, 26 March 1932, Crump Collection.

85. E. H. Crump to Watkins Overton, 21 March 1932, Crump Collection.

86. Franklin D. Roosevelt to E. H. Crump, 24 May 1932, Crump Collection.

87. E. H. Crump to Franklin D. Roosevelt, 27 May 1932, Crump Collection.

88. Address of Chairman James A. Farley of the Democratic National Committee at Nashville, Tennessee, 16 August 1934, Crump Collection; Dorsett, *Franklin D. Roosevelt and the City Bosses*, 37.

89. Franklin D. Roosevelt to E. H. Crump, 12 September 1932, Crump Collection.

90. *Memphis Evening Appeal*, 9 November 1932.

91. Ibid., 10 November 1932.

92. E. H. Crump to Frank Rice, 10 April 1933, Crump Collection.

93. E. H. Crump to M. A. McKinnon, 10 June 1932, Crump Collection.

94. Watkins Overton to E. H. Crump, 27 April 1932, Crump Collection.

95. Affidavit of Nat Wiseman, 19 July 1932, Crump Collection.

96. H. W. Pyle to Fiorello LaGuardia, 25 June 1932, Crump Collection.

97. H. W. Pyle to Herbert Hoover, 11 July 1932, Crump Collection.

98. J. B. Ellis, et al., to National Red Cross Headquarters, 11 July 1932, Crump Collection.

99. *Memphis Evening Appeal*, 19 July 1932.

100. Ibid., 20 July 1932.

101. E. H. Crump to William E. Borah, 26 July 1932, Crump Collection.

102. William E. Borah to E. H. Crump, 28 July 1932, Crump Collection.

103. Ibid., 16 August 1932, Crump Collection.

104. J. Roy Hickerson to G. Dave Wells, 26 May 1932, Crump Collection.

105. Watkins Overton to E. H. Crump, 28 January 1932, Crump Collection.

106. E. H. Crump to Watkins Overton, 23 May 1932, Crump Collection.

107. Ibid., 9 July 1932, Crump Collection.

108. *Memphis Evening Appeal*, 16 April 1932.

109. Ibid., 16 July 1932.

110. Sigafoos, *Cotton Row to Beale Street*, 166.

111. Lee, *Tennessee in Turmoil*, 135.

112. *Memphis Evening Appeal*, 4 August 1932.

113. Ibid.

114. Lee, *Tennessee in Turmoil*, 139.

115. *Memphis Evening Appeal*, 10 August 1932.

116. Lee, *Tennessee in Turmoil*, 140.

117. Biles, *Memphis in the Great Depression*, 84.

118. *Memphis Evening Appeal*, 22 October 1932.

119. Ibid., 21 December 1932; Watkins Overton, "To the People of Memphis from Watkins Overton, Mayor," *Memphis Evening Appeal*, 4 February 1933.

120. "Resolution Ordering a City Audit," 10 January 1933, Memphis Board of Commissioners Tickler Files, Shelby County Archives.

121. *Memphis Evening Appeal*, 4 February 1933.

122. Ibid., Watkins Overton to E. H. Crump, 11 February 1933, Crump Collection.

123. Ibid.

124. *Memphis Evening Appeal*, 10 January 1933.

125. Ibid., 18 January 1933.

126. Ibid., 16 March 1933.

127. Tom Love to E. H. Crump, 10 March 1933, Crump Collection.

128. *Memphis Evening Appeal*, 4 February 1933.

129. E. H. Crump to W. T. McLain, 12 February 1933, Crump Collection.

130. E. H. Crump to Watkins Overton, 24 February 1933, Crump Collection.

131. Watkins Overton to E. H. Crump, 3 March 1933, Crump Collection.

132. *Memphis Evening Appeal*, 5 May 1933; Watkins Overton to E. H. Crump, 13 May 1933, Crump Collection.

133. Watkins Overton to E. H. Crump, 13 May 1933, Crump Collection.

134. Ibid., 30 May 1933, Crump Collection; *Memphis Evening Appeal*, 30 May 1933.

135. *Memphis Evening Appeal*, 7 July 1933.

136. Ibid., 13 March 1933.

137. Ibid., 10 and 12 May 1933; Watkins Overton to E. H. Crump, 13 May 1933, Crump Collection.

138. *Memphis Commercial Appeal*, 6 June 1933.

139. *Memphis Evening Appeal*, 7 June 1933; Watkins Overton to E. H. Crump, 6 June 1933, Crump Collection.

140. E. H. Crump to W. T. McLain, 11 June 1933, Crump Collection.

"The Honor of Having No Opposition"

1. *Memphis Commercial Appeal*, 4 March 1934.

2. Ibid., 5 March 1934.

3. W. T. McLain to E. H. Crump, 25 January, 1934, Crump Collection.

4. Cordell Hull to E. H. Crump, 6 August 1934, Crump Collection.

5. Address of James A. Farley, 16 August 1934, Crump Collection.

6. Frank Rice to E. H. Crump, 17 March 1934, Crump Collection.

7. Ibid.; W. T. McLain to E. H. Crump, 17 March 1934, Crump Collection.

8. Assistant attorney general Will Gerber to W. T. McLain, 4 April 1934; W. T. McLain to E. H. Crump, 5 April 1934, Crump Collection.

9. *Memphis Commercial Appeal*, 22 May 1934.

10. E. H. Crump to Frank Rice, 26 March 1934, Crump Collection.

11. Ibid., 9 May 1934, Crump Collection.

12. Frank Rice to E. H. Crump, 7 June 1934; Watkins Overton to E. H. Crump, 18 June 1934, Crump Collection.

13. Watkins Overton to E. H. Crump, 13 August 1934, Crump Collection.

14. E. H. Crump to Italian ambassador Augusto Rosso, 8 June 1934; Augusto Rosso to E. H. Crump, 14 June 1934, Crump Collection.

15. "Some Conspicuous Examples of Foreign Born Americans Who Have Achieved Honor and Fame in America After Attaining Citizenship," 1934, Crump Collection.

16. Frank Rice to E. H. Crump, 7 June 1934, Crump Collection.

17. *Memphis Press-Scimitar*, 1 August 1934.

18. Statement on the Success of the Poll Tax Drive, 8 June 1934, Crump Collection.

19. *Memphis Press-Scimitar*, 3 August 1934.

20. *Memphis Commercial Appeal*, 3 August 1934.

21. Bobby Joe Williams, "Let There be Light: Tennessee Valley Authority Comes to Memphis," *West Tennessee Historical Society Papers* 30 (1976), 61–62; Biles, *Memphis in the Great Depression*, 80.

22. Owen P. White, "Sinners in Dixie," *Collier's*, 26 January 1935, 16, 43–44.

23. *Memphis Press-Scimitar*, 17 January, 1935.

24. White, "Sinners in Dixie," 43.

25. *Memphis Commercial Appeal*, 18 January 1935.

26. *Memphis Press-Scimitar*, 19 January 1935.

27. For a more detailed examination of Crump's attempt to smash organized crime, see G. Wayne Dowdy, "Sin in Memphis: Organized Crime and Machine Politics in a Southern City, 1935–1940," in Ted Olson, ed., *CrossRoads: A Southern Culture Annual* (Macon, GA: Mercer University Press, 2004), 171–93.

28. Linda McGregor Scott, "Machine Gun Kelly—A Return to Paradise," *West Tennessee Historical Society Papers* 50 (1996), 27.

29. *Memphis Press-Scimitar*, 17 December 1935.

30. *Memphis Commercial Appeal*, 22 June 1934.

31. Biles, *Memphis in the Great Depression*, 15; *Memphis Press-Scimitar* 31 March 1933.

32. *Memphis Press-Scimitar*, 22 June 1934.

33. *Memphis Commercial Appeal*, 21 January 1935.

34. Ibid.

35. *Memphis Commercial Appeal*, 4 March 1935.

36. Ibid., 3 March 1935.

37. Ibid.

38. Ibid.

39. *Memphis Commercial Appeal*, 4 March 1935.

40. Ibid., 3 March 1935.

41. Ibid.

42. *Memphis Commercial Appeal*, 22 June 1935.

43. *Memphis Press-Scimitar*, 5 March 1935.

44. Ibid., 25 April 1935.

45. Ibid., 17 June 1935; *Memphis Commercial Appeal*, 22 June 1935.

46. *Memphis Commercial Appeal*, 11 February 1935.

47. Ibid., 12 April 1935.

48. *Memphis-Press Scimitar*, 5 May 1935.

49. Ibid.

50. *Memphis Commercial Appeal*, 11 February 1935.

51. Ibid., 16 August 1935.

52. Ibid., 30 March 1935.

53. Ibid.

54. Ibid.

55. *Memphis Commercial Appeal*, 11 April 1935.

56. Ibid., 16 May 1935.

57. Ibid., 16 August 1935.

58. *Memphis Press-Scimitar*, 12 August 1935.

59. *Memphis Commercial Appeal*, 16 August 1935.

60. *Memphis Press-Scimitar*, 30 April 1936.

61. Ibid., 17 June 1935.

62. *Memphis Commercial Appeal*, 5 January 1936.

63. Memphis Police Department, Homicide Bureau Annual Report, 1934, Watkins Overton Papers, Memphis Public Library and Information Center.

64. *Memphis Commercial Appeal*, 5 January 1936.

65. Watkins Overton to Clifford Davis, 10 January 1935, Overton Papers.

66. W. T. Griffin to Watkins Overton, 2 February 1935, Overton Papers.

67. Watkins Overton to W. T. Griffin, 6 February 1935, Overton Papers.

68. *Memphis Commercial Appeal*, 5 January 1936.

69. Captain W. F. Glisson to Chief Inspector William T. Griffin, 30 March 1937, Overton Papers.

70. W. F. Glisson to William T. Griffin, 6 April 1937, Overton Papers.

71. Clifford Davis to Watkins Overton, 2 May 1936, Overton Papers.

72. Sergeant E. L. McCarty to Captain J. P. Cross, 2 April 1938, Overton Papers.

73. *Memphis Commercial Appeal*, 5 November 1935.

74. Ibid.

75. Democratic National Campaign Committee secretary Lawrence Wood Robert, Jr., to E. H. Crump, 28 July 1936, Crump Collection.

76. Miller, *Mr. Crump of Memphis*, 234–35.

77. Ibid.; Kenneth McKellar to E. H. Crump, 12 September 1936, Crump Collection.

78. James A. Farley to E. H. Crump, 15 August 1936, Crump Collection.

79. Ibid., 2 September 1936, Crump Collection.

80. E. H. Crump to James A. Farley, 3 September 1936, Crump Collection.

81. James A. Farley to Franklin Roosevelt, 7 October 1936, Crump Collection.

82. *The Public Papers and Addresses of Franklin D. Roosevelt* (New York: Random House, 1938), 481.

83. Betty Crump Pidgeon McGeorge, remarks given at the E. H. Crump Symposium, 23 October 2004.

84. 1953 Captains and Lieutenants List, Crump Collection.

85. Voter list, n. d., Crump Collection.

86. Ibid.

87. List of Citizens' Contributions, 22 October 1936; List of Contributions from the Attorney General's Office to the Democratic Campaign Fund, 1936; List of Contributions from the Mayor's Office, 6 October 1936, Crump Collection.

88. Campaign Contributions Report of the Street Cleaning Department, 1936, E. H. Crump Collection.

89. State Democratic finance director L. G. Durr to E. H. Crump, 3 November 1936, Crump Collection.

90. John B. Vesey to E. H. Crump with attached campaign advertisement script, 5 November 1936, Crump Collection.

91. *Memphis Commercial Appeal*, 5 November 1936.

92. Michael J. Webber, "Election of 1936" in Robert S. McElvaine, ed., *Encyclopedia of the Great Depression* (New York: Macmillan Reference USA, 2004), 285–289.

93. J. E. Walker to E. W. Hale with attached report to Democratic National Headquarters, 21 October 1940, E. W. Hale Collection, Memphis Public Library and Information Center; G. Wayne Dowdy, "'We Engaged in a Hard Campaign': Primary Sources Related to the 1940 and 1944 Presidential Elections in Shelby County, Tennessee," *Tennessee Librarian*, vol. 54, no. 1 (2003).

94. William R. Majors, *The End of Arcadia: Gordon Browning and Tennessee Politics* (Memphis: Memphis State University Press, 1982), 61.

95. Ibid., 70.

96. Watkins Overton to E. H. Crump, 30 June 1936, Crump Collection.

97. Report of Douglas Johnson and Van Hiler at the Conclusion of Tour of Middle Tennessee, Sunday, July 5, 1936, Crump Collection.

98. Majors, *The End of Arcadia*, 75–76.

99. Ibid., 77.

100. *Time*, 17 August 1936.

101. *Memphis Commercial Appeal*, 11 February 1937.

102. Ibid., 13 February 1937.

103. Patrick W. O'Daniel, "Memphis and the Ohio–Mississippi Valley Flood of 1937" (M.A. thesis, University of Memphis, 2003), 66.

104. Ibid., 66–67.

105. Cornelia Fredericks to C. T. Noel, 25 January 1937, Crump Collection.

106. E. H. Crump to Watkins Overton, 30 January 1937, Crump Collection.

107. Watkins Overton to E. H. Crump, 2 February 1937, Crump Collection.

108. Gulf Refining Company et al. to E. H. Crump, 29 January 1937, Crump Collection.

109. Cornelia Fredericks to Marvin Pope, 1 February 1937, Crump Collection.

110. O'Daniel, "Memphis and the Ohio–Mississippi Valley Flood of 1937," 106–7.

111. Ibid., 105–6.

112. Marvin Pope to E. H. Crump, 16 August 1937, Crump Collection.

113. *Memphis Commercial Appeal*, 21 August 1937.

"God Bless You, Boss"

1. Majors, *The End of Arcadia*, 97.

2. E. H. Crump to Gordon Browning, 23 April 1937, Crump Collection.

3. Majors, *The End of Arcadia*, 98.

4. Watkins Overton to E. H. Crump, 23 July 1937, Crump Collection.

5. Majors, *The End of Arcadia*, 98–99.

6. Miller, *Mr. Crump of Memphis*, 245.

7. Ibid., 243.

8. Memorandum on Gordon Browning, 1938, Crump Collection.

9. Majors, *The End of Arcadia*, 105.

10. Ibid, 108.

11. Ibid.

12. Majors, *The End of Arcadia*, 114.

13. J. Ross McKinney to E. H. Crump, 6 October 1937, Crump Collection.

14. E. H. Crump to Wardlow Steele, 5 May 1938, Crump Collection.

15. Majors, *The End of Arcadia*, 115–16.

16. Prentice Cooper to E. H. Crump, 7 March 1938, Crump Collection.

17. E. W. Hale, Statement on Voter Registration, 1938, Crump Collection.
18. Wardlaw Steele to E. H. Crump, 4 May 1938; E. H. Crump to Wardlaw Steele, 5 May 1938, Crump Collection.
19. Memorandum to Prentice Cooper, 1938, Crump Collection.
20. *Memphis Press-Scimitar*, 4 January 1938.
21. Ibid.
22. *Memphis Press-Scimitar*, 11 August 1938.
23. Ibid., 11 August 1938.
24. *Memphis Press-Scimitar*, 1 August 1936.
25. Ibid., 11 August 1936.
26. Majors, *The End of Arcadia*, 124.
27. *Memphis Press-Scimitar*, 11 August 1938.
28. *Memphis Commercial Appeal*, 5 July 1938.
29. *Memphis Press-Scimitar*, 29 December 1939.
30. E. H. Crump to Watkins Overton, 25 August 1938, Crump Collection.
31. W. W. Mallory to Watkins Overton, 30 April 1938, Crump Collection.
32. Watkins Overton to E. H. Crump, 2 May 1938, Crump Collection; *Memphis Press-Scimitar*, 23 November 1938.
33. *Memphis Commercial Appeal*, 1 October 1938.
34. Miller, *Mr. Crump of Memphis*, 262.
35. James Street, "Mista Crump Keeps Rollin' Along," *Collier's*, 9 April 1938, 16.
36. *Memphis Commercial Appeal*, 27 November 1938.
37. *Memphis Press-Scimitar*, 23 November 1938.
38. Ibid.
39. Miller, *Mr. Crump of Memphis*, 266.
40. Jonathan Daniels to E. H. Crump, 25 November 1938, Crump Collection.
41. Evelyn Humphreys to Jonathan Daniels, 28 November 1938, Crump Collection.
42. Jonathan Daniels to E. H. Crump, 7 December 1938, Crump Collection.
43. Evelyn Humphreys made the following notation on a December 5, 1938, letter from Daniels: "Mr. Daniels was in this a. m. had to be in Mps. & would come by. Called 12–8–38, Mr. Crump will not have time to get in on any outside matters at this time. Probably after the first of the year he will not be so tied up."
44. E. H. Crump to Jonathan Daniels, 10 December 1938, Crump Collection.
45. W. C. Handy, *Father of the Blues: An Autobiography* (New York: Da Capo Press, 1941), 93.

46. Beale Street Shieks (Stokes and Sane), "Mr. Crump Don't Like It," *Blues Masters, Volume 12: Memphis Blues* (Rhino Records R271129, 1993); Larry Nager, *Memphis Beat: The Lives and Times of America's Musical Crossroads* (New York: St. Martin's Press, 1998), 69.

47. Patrick W. O'Daniel, "Memphis and the Ohio–Mississippi Valley Flood of 1937," (M.A. thesis, University of Memphis, 2003), 26.

48. Memorandum of changes to *Saturday Evening Post* article, 1939, Crump Collection.

49. E. H. Crump to *Saturday Evening Post*, 13 February 1939, Crump Collection.

50. Jonathan Daniels, "He Suits Memphis," *Saturday Evening Post*, 10 June 1939, 22.

51. Ibid., 50.

52. *Memphis Commercial Appeal*, 3 March 1939; F. H. Gailor, "Memorandum on the Liquor Bill," 1939, Crump Collection.

53. Ibid.

54. Prentice Cooper to E. H. Crump, 5 July 1939, Crump Collection.

55. *Memphis Press-Scimitar*, 26 May 1939.

56. *Memphis Commercial Appeal*, 13 July 1939.

57. Scott Melton, "Machine Prince or Mayoral Pauper?: Watkins Overton's Political Relationship with Ed Crump and the Crump Machine," *West Tennessee Historical Society Papers* 49 (1995), 185.

58. *Memphis Commercial Appeal*, 24 August 1939.

59. Melton, "Machine Prince or Mayoral Pauper?" 185–86.

60. Walter Chandler to Marvin Pope, 17 August 1939, Chandler Papers.

61. Ibid.

62. Miller, *Mr. Crump of Memphis*, 272.

63. Justus D. Doenecke and John E. Wilz, *From Isolation to War, 1931–1941* (Arlington Heights: Harlan Davidson, 1991), 86–87.

64. Dowdy, "E. H. Crump and the Mayors of Memphis," 88.

65. Pat Harrison to E. H. Crump, 30 October 1939, Crump Collection.

66. *Memphis Press-Scimitar*, 2 October 1939.

67. Agenda of the Democratic Celebration-Fairgrounds, 20 September 1939, Crump Collection.

68. J. J. Brennan to E. H. Crump, 2 October 1939, Crump Collection.

69. Dowdy, "E. H. Crump and the Mayors of Memphis," 88.

70. Ibid., 89.

Afterword

1. Walter Chandler to E. H. Crump, 6 July 1940, Chandler Papers.
2. Roger Biles, "Robert R. Church, Jr., of Memphis: Black Republican Leader in the Age of Democratic Ascendancy, 1928–1940," *Tennessee Historical Quarterly* 42 (Winter 1983), 379; List of R. R. Church Property Seized by the City of Memphis, 1940, Crump Collection.
3. W. S. Martin to E. H. Crump, 1 November 1940, Crump Collection.
4. Biles, "Robert R. Church, Jr., of Memphis," 380.
5. J. E. Walker to E. W. Hale, 31 October 1940, Hale Collection.
6. Affidavit of Blair T. Hunt, 21 December 1943; affidavit of George W. Lee, 11 February 1944, Crump Collection.
7. Melton, "Blacks in Memphis, Tennessee," 220–21.
8. A. Philip Randolph to E. H. Crump, 6 April 1944, Crump Collection.
9. Dowdy, "Censoring Popular Culture," 108.
10. Dowdy, "E. H. Crump and the Mayors of Memphis," 93.
11. Dowdy, "Censoring Popular Culture," 109.
12. J. Strom Thurmond to E. H. Crump, 16 August 1948, Crump Collection.
13. *Chicago Tribune*, 2 April 1939.
14. *The Economist*, 21 August 1943.
15. *Time*, 27 May 1946, 20.
16. *Chicago Defender*, 8 April 1944.
17. Melvin G. Holli, *The American Mayor: The Best and Worst Big-City Leaders* (University Park: Pennsylvania State University Press, 1999), 4–8.
18. Ibid., 35–38.
19. Ibid., 12–16.
20. Peter J. O'Malley, "Anton J. Cermak," in Melvin G. Holli and Peter d' A. Jones, eds., *Biographical Dictionary of American Mayors, 1820–1980* (Westport: Greenwood Press, 1981), 60–61.
21. Paul M. Green, "Anton J. Cermak: The Man and His Machine," in Paul M. Green and Melvin G. Holli, eds., *The Mayors: The Chicago Political Tradition* (Carbondale: Southern Illinois University Press, 1995), 99–110.

Bibliography

Manuscript Collections

Walter Chandler Papers, Memphis Public Library and Information Center

Everett R. Cook Oral History Collection, Memphis Public Library and Information Center

E. H. Crump Collection, Memphis Public Library and Information Center

E. W. Hale Collection, Memphis Public Library and Information Center

Kenneth McKellar Collection, Memphis Public Library and Information Center

Watkins Overton Collection, University of Memphis

Watkins Overton Papers, Memphis Public Library and Information Center

Roane Waring Collection, Memphis Public Library and Information Center

Government Documents

Memphis Board of Commissioners, Loose Papers, 1910–1940, Shelby County Archives

Memphis Board of Commissioners, Minute Books, 1910–1940, Shelby County Archives

Memphis Board of Commissioners, *One Year and Eight Months under Commission Government* (Memphis, 1911), E. H. Crump Collection, Memphis Public Library and Information Center

Louise Gambill, *Memphis in the Heart of the Mid-South: A Story of Progress Made Possible by Taxes* (Memphis, 1935), Memphis Public Library and Information Center

Memphis Legislative Council, Loose Papers, 1909, Shelby County Archives

Municipal Reference Library, *Municipal Progress in Memphis* (Memphis, 1937),
    Memphis Public Library and Information Center

Newspapers

Chicago Defender
Chicago Tribune
Memphis Commercial Appeal
Memphis Evening Appeal
Memphis News–Scimitar
Memphis Press–Scimitar
New York Times

Books

Biles, Roger. *Memphis in the Great Depression*. Memphis: Memphis State
    University Press, 1986.
Bolin, James Duane. *Bossism and Reform in a Southern City: Lexington,
    Kentucky, 1880–1940*. Lexington: University Press of Kentucky, 2000.
Bond, Beverly G., and Janann Sherman. *Memphis in Black and White*.
    Charleston: Arcadia, 2003.
Bradley, Robert Rice. *Progressive Cities: The Commission Government
    Movement in America, 1901–1920*. Austin: University of Texas Press, 1977.
Bruce, Andrew A., and Thomas S. Fitzgerald. *A Study of Crime in the City of
    Memphis, Tennessee*. Chicago: Northwestern University Press, 1928.
Burner, David. *Herbert Hoover: A Public Life*. New York: Knopf, 1979.
Doenecke, Justus D., and John E. Wilz. *From Isolation to War, 1931–1941*.
    Arlington Heights: Harlan Davidson, 1991.
Dorsett, Lyle W. *Franklin D. Roosevelt and the City Bosses*. Port Washington:
    Kennikat Press, 1977.
———. *The Pendergast Machine*. New York: Oxford University Press, 1968.
Green, Paul M., and Melvin G. Holli, eds. *The Mayors: The Chicago Political
    Tradition*. Carbondale: Southern Illinois University Press, 1995.
Handy, W. C. *Father of the Blues: An Autobiography*. New York: Da Capo
    Press, 1941.
Holli, Melvin G. *The American Mayor: The Best and Worst Big-City Leaders*.
    University Park: Pennsylvania State University Press, 1999.

Holli, Melvin G., and Peter d'A. Jones, eds. *Biographical Dictionary of American Mayors, 1820–1980.* Westport: Greenwood Press, 1981.

Irish, Ann B. *Joseph W. Byrns of Tennessee.* Knoxville: University of Tennessee Press, 2001.

Jackson, Kenneth T. *The Ku Klux Klan in the City, 1915–1930.* New York: Oxford University Press, 1967.

Kennedy, David M. *Freedom from Fear: The American People in Depression and War, 1929–1945.* New York: Oxford University Press, 1999.

Lamon, Lester C. *Black Tennesseans, 1900–1930.* Knoxville: University of Tennessee Press, 1977.

Langsdon, Phillip. *Tennessee: A Political History.* Franklin: Hillboro Press, 2000.

Lee, David D. *Tennessee in Turmoil: Politics in the Volunteer State, 1920–1932.* Memphis: Memphis State University Press, 1979.

Lewis, Selma S. *A Biblical People in the Bible Belt: The Jewish Community of Memphis, Tennessee, 1840s–1960s.* Macon: Mercer University Press, 1998.

Majors, William R. *The End of Arcadia: Gordon Browning and Tennessee Politics.* Memphis: Memphis State University Press, 1982.

McElvaine, Robert S. ed. *Encyclopedia of the Great Depression.* New York: Macmillan Reference USA, 2004.

Miller, William D. *Memphis during the Progressive Era, 1900–1917.* Memphis: Memphis State University Press, 1957.

———. *Mr. Crump of Memphis.* Baton Rouge: Louisiana State University Press, 1964.

Nager, Larry. *Memphis Beat: The Lives and Times of America's Musical Crossroads.* New York: St. Martin's Press, 1998.

Neal, Steve. *Happy Days Are Here Again: The 1932 Democratic Convention, the Emergence of FDR and How America Was Changed Forever.* New York: William Morrow, 2004.

Roosevelt, Franklin D. *The Public Papers and Addresses of Franklin D. Roosevelt.* New York: Random House, 1938.

Sigafoos, Robert A. *Cotton Row to Beale Street: A Business History of Memphis.* Memphis: Memphis State University Press, 1979.

Tucker, David M. *Lieutenant Lee of Beale Street.* Nashville: Vanderbilt University Press, 1971.

———. *Memphis Since Crump: Bossism, Blacks, and Civic Reformers, 1948–1968.* Knoxville: University of Tennessee Press, 1980.

Van West, Carroll, ed. *The Tennessee Encyclopedia of History and Culture.*
Nashville: Tennessee Historical Society, 1998.

Walk, Joe. *Memphis Executive and Legislative Government.* Memphis: 1996.

Wilson, Charles Reagan, and William Ferris, eds. *Encyclopedia of Southern Culture.* Chapel Hill: University of North Carolina Press, 1989.

Yellin, Carol Lynn, and Janann Sherman. *The Perfect 36: Tennessee Delivers Woman Suffrage.* Memphis: Serviceberry Press, 1998.

Articles

Biles, Roger. "Robert R. Church, Jr., of Memphis: Black Republican Leader in the Age of Democratic Ascendancy, 1928–1940." *Tennessee Historical Quarterly* 42 (Winter 1983).

Bridges, Lamar Whitlow. "Editor Mooney Versus Boss Crump." *West Tennessee Historical Society Papers* 20 (1966).

Daniels, Jonathan. "He Suits Memphis." *Saturday Evening Post*, June 10, 1939.

Dowdy, G. Wayne. "'A Business Government by a Business Man': E. H. Crump as a Progressive Mayor, 1910–1915." *Tennessee Historical Quarterly*, Fall 2001.

———. "Censoring Popular Culture: Political and Social Control in Segregated Memphis." *West Tennessee Historical Society Papers* 55 (2001).

———. "E. H. Crump and the Mayors of Memphis." *West Tennessee Historical Society Papers* 53 (1999).

———. "Expansion of the Crump Machine: Politics in Shelby County, 1928–1936." *West Tennessee Historical Society Papers* 56 (2002).

———. "Sin in Memphis: Organized Crime and Machine Politics in a Southern City, 1935–1940." In *CrossRoads: A Southern Culture Annual*, edited by Ted Olson. Macon, GA: Mercer University Press, 2004.

———. "'The People Have Made Their Statement': The Bellomini Payoff Book and the 1927 Memphis City Election." *Arkansas Review: A Journal of Delta Studies* (December 2004).

———. "'We Engaged in a Hard Campaign': Primary Sources Related to the 1940 and 1944 Presidential Elections in Shelby County, Tennessee." *Tennessee Librarian* 54, no. 1 (2003).

Frye, William H. "For Their Exclusive Enjoyment: Racial Politics and the Founding of Douglass Park, Memphis, 1910–1913." *West Tennessee Historical Society Papers* 47 (1993).

Grantham, Dewey W. "Tennessee and Twentieth-Century American Politics."
    In *Tennessee History: The Land, the People, and the Culture*, edited by Carroll
    Van West. Knoxville: University of Tennessee Press, 1998.

Hepler, Richard W. "Bovine Tuberculosis and the Battle for Pure Milk in
    Memphis, 1910–1911." *West Tennessee Historical Society Papers* 40 (1986).

Kitchens, Allen H. "Ouster of Edward H. Crump, 1915–1916." *West Tennessee
    Historical Society Papers* 19 (1965).

Melton, Scott. "Machine Prince or Mayoral Pauper?: Watkins Overton's
    Political Relationship with Ed Crump and the Crump Machine." *West
    Tennessee Historical Society Papers* 44 (1995).

Phillips, Virginia. "Rowlett Paine, Mayor of Memphis, 1920–1924." *West
    Tennessee Historical Society Papers* 13 (1959).

Scott, Linda McGregor. "Machine Gun Kelly–a Return to Paradise." *West
    Tennessee Historical Society Papers* 50 (1996).

Street, James. "Mista Crump Keeps Rollin' Along." *Collier's*, 9 April 1938.

Velie, Lester. "You Can't See that Movie: Censorship in Action." *Collier's*,
    6 May 1950.

Walker, Randolph Meade. "The Role of the Black Clergy in Memphis." *West
    Tennessee Historical Society Papers* 33 (1979).

White, Owen P. "Sinners in Dixie." *Collier's*, 26 January 1935.

White, Paul. "The Life and Career of Walter Chandler." *West Tennessee
    Historical Society Papers* 53 (1999).

Williams, Bobby Joe. "Let There Be Light: Tennessee Valley Authority Comes
    to Memphis." *West Tennessee Historical Society Papers* 30 (1976).

Dissertations and Theses

Adkins, Walter P. "Beale Street Goes to the Polls." MA thesis, Ohio State
    University, 1935.

Caplinger, Christopher. "Conflict and Community: Racial Segregation in a
    New South City, 1860–1914." PhD diss., Vanderbilt University, 2003.

Melton, Gloria Brown. "Blacks in Memphis, Tennessee, 1920–1955." PhD diss.,
    Washington State University, 1982.

O'Daniel, Patrick W. "Memphis and the Ohio–Mississippi Valley Flood of
    1937." MA thesis, University of Memphis, 2003.

Index

149